M000086135

Cover by: Fiona Jayde

ISBN 978-1980819622
ISBN eBook **978-1986879767**

Library of Congress Control Number: 2018904895

Thank you
For Registering @
empowher

Dedicated to my great-grandmother, who endured, and to my grandmother, who persevered. I wish, like Outlander, I could time travel to your world.

To all the passive girls: You have a voice... Speak up!

To my children, who are screaming right now! Thank you for teaching me how to block out unnecessary noise.

A note to the reader:

Let's get real for a second! The book is to share with you my journey and struggles. All stories in the book are authentic experiences that occurred in my life. I do not include any real names and descriptions of anyone I have worked with and the events that occurred happened many years ago and probably don't reflect what is happening now. None of my opinions and things that I have learned are the reflection of current or past employers. All views are strictly my own.

Contents

Introduction

Women working together for one goal: Build. Strong women who collaborate: Thrive in adversity!

Growing up as a small child in the 1980s I had the privilege of watching some of the best superhero movies and cartoons. From She-Rah's bravery and Scooby Doo solving mysteries to Transformers and Jem and Holograms, my world was filled with make believe. One of the things I loved was reading comic books, such as Archie Comics, Marvel, and DC. I would watch Christopher Reeve as Superman on repeat and I always wanted to be Lois Lane. I was mesmerized by her tenacity and quick wit along with her ability to outsmart any man in the room without breaking a sweat.

Then I was introduced to the 1984 Supergirl movie and I was in superhero heaven. I remember sitting and watching this young beautiful blond transform into a female superhero; a real-life superman for girls! I wanted her blonde hair gracefully flipped with every turn and punch; her short red skirt, and her strength. Basically, I wanted to be this woman hero. As a little girl I knew from the beginning I never wanted to be the villain; the jealous person who tries to seek revenge; the mean girl. I wanted to be the superhero, like Supergirl! I wanted to be nice but tough; a leader with a heart; an honest girl who liked comic books and Transformers and would always do the right thing.

Supergirl (in the 1984 film), also known as Kara Zor-El, is from an isolated Kryptonian world and is thrown in to an unknown world called Earth. Her cousin is Superman, or Kal-El, and she must find the one thing that powers Argo City, which is called the Omegahedron. Wonder Woman was another TV show I watched and was mesmerized with. In the 2017 Wonder Woman movie, she is also taken from her Amazonian upbringing and transported into our world. One of the things I admire most about Supergirl and Wonder Woman is that they travel to an unknown world, a place they are not familiar with, and even if they stumbled or failed, they never gave up. They instead use their skills and remain confident that they will find their way through the unfamiliar world.

It appears all superheroes face a provisional phase where they go through a specific situation that refines their strength and an event that helps define who they will become: Will they become a villain or remain true to their heart as someone who saves lives? In any leadership role, you must remember to try to emulate what a woman superhero stands for. Use your superpower skills for good and not to tear someone down; be the shield for your staff and colleagues. In other words, when a staff member does something wrong, don't point fingers at them, instead try to help fix the problem and learn from the mistake while moving forward. Use your skills and reputation to elevate other women, to help them climb in their careers instead of using them as steps to further your own. The chief chemist in Wonder Woman was a female, Isabel Moru, who used her knowledge and skills to create a deadly mustard gas instead of using her genius to help those around her. I guess in all worlds we have our villains, how else will we learn to form thicker skin and truly learn about ourselves?

In the Amazonian world that Wonder Woman came from, also known as Diana Prince, it was an all-female island that Zeus created to protect the Amazonians from mankind. These women helped each other in every aspect of life, and as I watched the 2017 Wonder Woman movie, I wished that all women could work together the way these women helped and protected one another. I also believe that Patty Jenkins, the female director of the 2017 Wonder Woman movie brought the iconic heroine in a more vulnerable light.

The world of comics has a long history, but it seems that comic heroines often start in the jungle. Until comic book artist Fletcher Hanks created Fantomah, the Mystery Jungle Woman in 1940, there weren't any female superheroes in the comic book world. According to an article by Steven Schneider, Fantomah used her supernatural powers to punish those who would threaten the jungle or its inhabitants. Then came Sheena, Queen of the Jungle, who was introduced to the world before Wonder Woman in 1937. She was not only an expert in combat and weapons handling, but also able to speak with animals.

Each woman superhero has her heroic traits that differentiate her from men, and as women we should never compare ourselves to men; because like Wonder Woman or Supergirl we have other skills that give us an advantage. Wonder Woman shielded the men behind her during the World War I battle scene, where she charged across "no man's land" to save a village, and that is a scene that my daughter will never forget. A Woman; the shield; and men huddling behind her! But at the same time, it teaches us about being a team player and knowing that a good team will make you more powerful in the end, which is why honesty and integrity are always superhero traits that we must cherish. Having humility and bravery during battle, or in our case when we are trying to climb that corporate ladder, are more powerful than they may first appear. Climb the ladder but make sure you are not hurting innocent people along the way. In the battle of the corporate world you must be fierce and embrace ambition but do it with tact and never hide the fact that you want to grow and thrive. Even Supergirl and Wonder Woman lost minor battles, but they persevered, learned from their mistakes, and moved on.

In this book you can be Wonder Woman or even a Supergirl in your own world, but you must also know that reality weighs in and we cannot do it all. Even

Wonder Woman wanted a balanced life, but for her, saving lives and doing the right thing always came first. We want it all as women, and I'm sorry to spoil it, but we can't have it all. We have to make sacrifices the way our heroines do, or we will be exhausted, anxious, and setting ourselves up for failure.

A superhero thrown into the unknown world must always find their way, grow, and save others in the process. This is the same way I felt when I was thrown into the college life, the unknown; and later thrown into the real world without a clue of what I "should" be doing.

It's OK to not know what you want to be when you grow up!

It's OK to not know what you want to major in!

Know that you can be uncertain!

You will still be successful.

I graduated from high school in May of 1997 and was ecstatic to start my venture out in the real world. Yet, the scary part for me was when signing up at our local community college I had to declare a major. *What?* I didn't even know what I was going to have for dinner that night, how was I supposed to know what I wanted to be? I thought, the best option for me was to major in psychology because I loved the study of the human psyche...but then I took my first psychology course and I hated the class. I also didn't like the fact that I had to take a lot of math and science courses. My first year in college was spent just trying to rack up my prerequisite courses, primarily math and science, so I could transfer out of community college and into a good university. I felt lost at times because I didn't know what career I wanted to go into, I was only in Psychology because I HAD to declare something, but did I really want to spend my entire life pursuing that career? I loved anthropology courses and took the easy way out of taking a science lab class needed to transfer, which was anthropology lab. I thrived in the English courses, history classes, and Shakespeare courses, however, I never took any journalism because I had already completed similar courses in high school.

When I finally transferred out of community college and got accepted to Cal Poly, San Luis Obispo, I transferred as a psychology major and still didn't know what I was doing, perpetually flabbergasted as to why I just didn't declare "No Major" from the beginning. I didn't know what I was doing, and that is perfectly okay! I thought that once I transferred to Cal Poly, I could switch majors easily and I would know what I wanted to focus on, however I quickly found out how wrong I was. At Cal Poly, I took a lot of communication courses and fell in love with the major right away, but, at Cal Poly they made it very difficult to switch majors. I had to get signature of the psychology department dean to switch over to communications and then needed the communications department dean's signature to allow me to switch. He didn't want to sign the papers because I had not taken all the required prerequisites to be in the communication major...so by the second semester there, I started taking all the necessary communication prerequisite courses to switch majors and prompt the dean to sign my transfer paper. It was not as easy of a process as I had thought!

Why would any college not allow students to switch majors easily? I remember thinking. *Some of us, like me, are lost and don't know what the hell we want to be when we grow up! Isn't college supposed to be a time to experience new things and delve into the unknown until we know what we want?* At that time, I wasn't sure why the process of changing majors was such an arduous procedure at Cal Poly, nevertheless, I did everything I could to make sure I got the best out of my experience. From interning at a morning radio station at 5am to holding a position at an NBC news affiliate broadcasting station as a marketing assistant, I wanted to see what I was good at, and more importantly, what I didn't like doing. I also worked on the school paper and wrote a few articles, but found out later that I didn't enjoy journalism as I did in high school; it became too political at times (even at a college newspaper). By the end of my first year at Cal Poly I relished in the courses I was taking as a communications major, especially those being taught by professors who were already in the field and brought field experience to the classroom. One of my professors was a CNN correspondent who, at that time, did not have an assignment and was teaching us instead. He was wonderful to listen to because he was enthusiastic about his job in broadcasting and teaching us how to be in front of a camera, giving us tips and tricks we'd never learn from a textbook.

My public relations instructor took my love for writing and helped me realize that public relations and marketing was where my true passion existed. Another instructor that I thoroughly enjoyed having was my graphic and interpersonal communications professor, who taught me about all the unfairness in the world and made me explore my creative side in ways I'd never experienced. When the dean of the communications department would still not sign my papers to switch my major because I was short a class, it was this professor who took the time to have a meaningful talk with me and I will never forget what he said.

My professor told me that sometimes the world around us doesn't always work to our advantage and we have to make things happen for ourselves with the word "NO" never being an option. He told me that he saw something special in me the first day of class, and I needed to pursue other college options and think about transferring out of Cal Poly.

I transferred that semester to University of the Pacific as a communications major and I thrived like never before. I loved my major, I loved what I was studying, and more importantly, at Pacific my instructors were just as nurturing as my interpersonal communication professor was at Cal Poly, if not more. Dr. Mom from Pacific was an amazing teacher that taught us ethics and the value of being a good, responsible public relations professional and to never compromise our morals.

I was lost during the first couple of years in college, starting out at community college in a major I wasn't interested in, transferring with that major to Cal Poly, wanting to switch majors, etc. But, I persevered, and I never gave up on finding my passion! What worked for me was trying to be involved in as many things as possible to find out what exactly that passion was. The struggle to find my place and the quest to find what I loved was very difficult at times and I often felt like giving up. I remember sitting outside my school building at Cal Poly and sobbing because I didn't know what road was ahead of me. I was still lost in this big campus with a small-town community, but I eventually found myself at University of the Pacific and knew I was on the right path.

With my father's help (and the help of some delicious baklava that he brought with him), we met with the admissions counselor at Pacific and she made the transition very smooth. It may have taken me five years to finish my bachelor's degree, but my last year was the most important because I finally knew where I was going with my studies and where I wanted to go afterwards.

About eighty percent of students in the United States end up changing their major at least once, according to the National Center for Education Statistics, that is nearly 4 out of 5! On average, college students change their major at least three times over the course of their college career. "Research and be ahead of the game," says Fritz Grupe, the creator of mymajors.com and an emeritus professor of computer science at the University of Nevada. "You may not know what to do with the rest of your life at age 18, but you can cover your bases with prudent planning." He states that some majors have a curriculum that follows a tight sequence of courses; therefore, it's easier to switch out of engineering than it is to take it up (if that's possible at all) later in your college career. The "biggest mistake" students make, Dr. Grupe adds, is failing to research what's required of the major, and the profession, that they choose to pursue. Nursing may sound attractive because "you like to help people," he says, but nursing students take the same demanding math and science curriculum as pre-med students, and the work is often very technical and not for every kind-hearted soul who just wants to be a caretaker.

Researching majors is crucial but remember to also look into what that major might bring to your career path. Getting a job right after college can be strenuous and overwhelming at times because you are now in the "real world," and that can be quite a shock after many years of college. You have to adult, and sometimes adulting can be much harder than you ever expected.

It's also OK to change jobs in your 20s, actually it's ok to change career paths at any age! Yet in your 20s this is the time in your life where you can explore different options in careers, finding the perfect fit of occupation since you will be working for the rest of your life until you retire, and you need to be doing something that makes you happy. Why would you be in a situation that makes you miserable for most of your life?

I teach at our local community college and in the last few months, I have had three students confide in me that they feel lost. They feel lost at work and are not sure what major to choose as their focus and what career path to take. My advice to them and to you is to take your time! Don't rush into life! You have your entire youth and your 20s to figure it out. Sometimes even those in their late 30s and 40s still haven't figured it out and change careers, and there is absolutely nothing wrong with this. I tell them to take as many classes as possible to find out what they enjoy, because happiness is paramount. Make sure you set a goal for yourself, so you are not a "professional student" and graduate at a decent time because it is expensive to go to school. Intern at jobs to get a feel for the environment and understand the working structures of that career.

One day it will click! And when that click happens you will see all the possibilities in front of you.

Obstacles will come your way, and as a woman in the workforce, you will also find yourself in many situations that you probably didn't think about in college. Being a working mom has its struggles, yet so does the decision about being a stay-at-home-mom; but those are decisions that you will have to make as a woman and as a family. The reality is, there is no one that can replace you as a mother and a mother's care is the most precious gift you can give to your children, therefore, no matter what you choose in life, as long as your children are happy and kind humans, you should not put too much pressure on yourself.

After finishing my doctorate program, I never imagined writing a book after writing my dissertation. But, after listening to my students for the last ten years and talking to my employees, hearing about their struggles, the notion that "women can do it all" needs to be in the forefront of conversations for young females. Is it a myth? Or can women really do it all?

It is my belief that many women think that having it all refers to having a career, relationship, children, looking great, going to the gym, having a social life outside of work and home, community service, all the while trying to maintain an emotionally healthy lifestyle. We cannot do it all, because we will run ourselves crazy thinking we can. Although, I do not mean to degrade the women who are "doing it all," and their definition could be different from the one I'm explaining, every woman's version of "all" is different depending on who you ask. There are many women who work part time or are stay-at-home mothers who run a business from their home, therefore, their perspective is different, and they may define themselves as "having it all." Other women who have executive positions and manage their home life also believe they have it all. Yet, once you become a parent, there are significant choices you must make in adjusting work and life. It means maybe giving up on community service efforts after work, or not attending after work functions. I see many college girls chasing the same dream I had, which was the "having it all" motto, but we need to educate them and help them make the best decisions for themselves, as I was not educated in this and had to learn a lot of things the hard way.

In an interview conducted with Joanna Pomykala, an executive at LinkedIn, and myself, she states that women should not try to do everything by themselves. "I am hyper-efficient with my time and I prioritize my family above work. I need to make sure I can be present with my children when I am with them, and leave work aside at those times."

Pomykala, also notes that she has a great support system at home and "I lean on my husband, my family and have been fortunate to have great child care. I am also grateful to work in a role and at a company that offers me some flexibility outside traditional 9-5 work hours to let me better balance my work & life needs. I acknowledge that not everyone is in a similar position, but you can't be afraid to ask for help at home as well as at work when you need it. You also have to prioritize paid help (e.g. childcare) in your budget and cut out other spending to make this happen. A support infrastructure doesn't happen by itself, you have to consciously build and invest in it."

Christine Hassler from the Huffington Post stated in an article that "A lot of women define Feminism as a woman's ability and right to have it all. But Feminism is not about having it all or doing it all. Feminism is about the freedom to make choices. Somewhere along the path of the women's liberation movement, we began to buy into the belief that to be an empowered woman means we have to do everything that both men and women do."

Pomykala has also been involved in an initiative to get more women into senior leadership positions at LinkedIn. The company is putting in significant efforts to have a more diverse and inclusive workforce. "However just because women are at the table, doesn't mean they speak up. Being aware of unconscious communication patterns is key to inclusive leadership. Many people assume that those who speak up in meetings are more interested in or knowledgeable about a topic and may wonder why others don't say anything. A lot of this may be due to people's personalities and communication styles – e.g. extroverts are more likely to speak out than introverts, but that doesn't mean introverts don't have great ideas to share. They just may need more time, more direct encouragement, or different communication channels to make their voices heard. And there are always people who tend to interrupt others, frequently this is men speaking over women. It's important to pay attention to communication patterns like this and intervene to make sure everyone on a team has a chance to speak their minds and make their voices heard."

As I have stated, we have different qualities than men that we can utilize to our advantage, and as women, we do have the freedom now more than ever to make choices. Yet, we still struggle because corporate America could be more flexible with working mothers to be able to have a more balanced lifestyle. Many American women are leaving the workforce because babysitting costs are extremely high, and it makes more sense to just stay home with their children, therefore, the company is losing out on these successful and innovative women. Companies should restructure how they see new moms: They need to look at new moms not as collateral damage, but as an opportunity to foster a better flexible schedule outside of the typical 8 - 5 clock in and clock out mentality to eliminate the high turnover rate.

The first chapter of this book deals with women in the workplace and how to deal with toxic bosses. Each chapter focuses on how we can overcome obstacles and these lessons are geared towards inspiring young girls to help them become great leaders in our community:

Maternity laws and HR ("Oh Mother"), being empowered within yourself ("Be Empowered"), the corporate environment and struggles of climbing the ladder ("The Battlefield"), the importance of branding yourself properly through social media ("The War Zone: Social Media"), and making excellent first impressions stick ("The First You").

This book is not designed around telling you what to do or as a biography about myself. Hell, I don't know anything, I'm still learning! Although, many of the stories I will share were my struggles during my learning process, I don't want this book to tell you how to juggle a career and life like I've had to do. I am writing this book for any young female who feels lost and doesn't know what the next step is. I am writing this book for the young female who is struggling to find herself in the real world and does not know how to handle a toxic work environment. I am writing this book for the young female who keeps asking herself "what am I doing?" I am also writing this book for the young woman who needs to understand that women who work together build more and women who collaborate are more innovative and successful.

These are my opinions and the events that I share is how I felt at the time.

We, as women need to stop the jealousy, insecure high school drama within the workplace, because there is room for growth for everyone. We, as women, must learn, now more than ever, to empower each other and understand what each woman is going through. It is important to teach young girls to be leaders who embody humbleness and kindness, be educators in their field who can embrace the generation after them and become motivators in a movement of women embracing other women.

The Villainous Authority

I remember receiving my acceptance letter from Cal Poly, San Luis Obispo in the fall of 1999. My mother was sitting on the couch with my two younger brothers as I eagerly opened the big white manila envelope, certain of its contents but needing to read the actual words before I could celebrate. I took out the pamphlet and letter, reading aloud that I had been accepted to Cal Poly, yet as my mother stood listening to my proclamation with a slight smile on her face, I knew deep inside that she wasn't ready to let go of her oldest child, to give me up to the outside world.

She hugged me and congratulated me, but it wasn't with all her heart, as it is not easy for a traditional Assyrian family to have their children leave the home. I was the first generation to be born and raised in America, educated in America and move away from home. My parents, who were born and raised in Iraq, came from a traditional Assyrian Christian background where things were done very differently. My mother was born in Dora, Iraq in the late 1950's and grew up in a time where many women didn't go beyond a high school education in the

Middle East. Most Assyrian women found husbands and raised their children in traditional homes without emphasizing education. As my grandparents made the decision to leave Iraq in the late 1970s, they first migrated to Spain, and then moved the family to Chicago, before officially moving to California. My mother moved with her father to California first to get everything situated for her mother, brother and sister, but eventually my mom enrolled in the same community college that I attended after high school and was set to study engineering, as she enjoyed mathematics and science. With a little over a year into her studies she met my father, eloped with him (as my grandparents didn't approve of my father at the time since he had been married and already had a child), and dropped out of college. With her education being put on hold, she became pregnant with me and became a stay-at-home mother for the next 15 years.

Growing up in a traditional Assyrian home meant I missed out on some fun things that my friends were able to do, such as spending the night at my friends' houses, going to prom, or attending after football game dances. My siblings and I had strict parents and our Christian beliefs played a huge role in how we were raised, such as attending Catholic school from elementary through 8th grade. Those that don't know who the Assyrian people are, we come from Nineveh, Iraq. The Assyrian Empire ruled for centuries in what now known as the Middle East, thousands of years before Christ.   The Assyrian nation was crippled with the death of our King, Ashurbanipal in 627 A.D. The great Assyrian cities of Ashur, Kalhu, and Nineveh are taken over by Medes, Babylonians, and the Persian army. Babylon rules over Assyrian regions for years and the great Babylonian King Hammurabi builds the walls of Babylon and Assyrian king Sennacherib   later   builds   the   Hanging Gardens of Babylon and orchestrates the modern use of an irrigation system for the plants called aqueducts inscribed to Sennacherib. According to Dalya Alberge in an article called *"Babylon's hanging garden: ancient scripts give clue to missing wonder"* written in The Gaurdian, these were part of a "80-kilometer (50 mi) series of canals, dams, and aqueducts used to carry water to Nineveh with water-raising screws used to raise it to the upper levels of the gardens."

Assyrians invented many things, and one being the wheel; library; postal service; iron weapons and so much more. Our language was spoken by Jesus, which at that time was called Aramaic. The Assyrians ruled the world for many centuries and were the first to accept Christianity; our oldest church, the Holy Apostolic Catholic Assyrian Church of the East, was formed in 2 AD.

My parents instilled rules for all of their children but a lot stricter of rules on my sister and I. Despite the stricter rules for their female children, I have never felt that it affected us in any negative way. Looking back, I remember feeling frustrated, but now I feel that they did us a service. They had the same expectations for all four of us children, although my two younger brothers seemed to get away with many things that my sister and I probably were not able to do, such as going to parties in high school, high school dances, and getting home past 10 pm. Yet, we were all encouraged to go to school, play sports, get chores done and engage in extracurricular activities. My younger brothers were groomed to be more athletic and my father coached their soccer teams. Possibly because my sister and I played sports, we were both raised to be strong women and to believe that girls could do anything boys could do. My mother emphasized education and would always tell us that finishing college is a major priority. She never pushed the traditional Assyrian agenda of getting her daughters married right away. She wanted her daughters to be educated first and find jobs that would make them not only thrive in their careers, but to make a difference in the lives of others.

My beautiful mother and myself at two years old.

Growing up my sister and I were complete opposites, she was a lot more talkative, personable, and not shy about letting people know how she felt. I, on the other hand, was quieter, didn't make friends easy, and was very passive in most social settings. My passive personality worried my mom, and most of the time my sister, who is younger than me, would defend me if someone said something negative towards me. My voice was there, and I knew what I wanted, but I didn't know how to express myself in the way my sister did so easily. At home, I was nurturing towards my younger siblings, as I was the oldest and had more responsibilities than they did. I would take charge and make sure we all had tasks to do as we played "teacher" in my bedroom. I would be the teacher and my sister and two younger brothers would be the students, and I assigned homework, gave tests, and made sure they finished any tasks I gave them on time. So you see, at home I was comfortable and knew exactly how to get what I wanted, but out in the real world my voice was lost inside my social anxiety.

"It took me quite a long time to develop a voice, and now that I have it, I am not going to be silent." -Madeleine Albright

It took me a long while to find my voice, but now that I have it I refuse to let it be silenced.

One of the greatest gifts my mother gave my sister and myself was teaching us that we could do anything we set our minds to. At one point in high school I wanted to go to design school in San Francisco, but even though my father didn't encourage the idea, my mother pushed for me to do what I was passionate about. My father would encourage us to be doctors, lawyers, or for me a news reporter, which are great professions...but I soon realized I needed to do what I thrived in and that was writing; specifically, being creative and marketing.

"I think women are foolish to pretend they are equal to men they are far superior and always have been."
~ William Golding, author of Lord of the Flies

Women, don't EVER think that you must be equal to a man. There is no such thing! Women have different skill sets than men, such as multitasking or the ability to tolerate pain better, I mean we do give birth for God's sake and God knew then who was the stronger gender. To all the women who fought for our rights before us, those that paved the way for us to vote, to go to school and to work, we must not disappoint them, even though times may have changed. Successful and professional women don't need to compete with men, but we must embrace our inner strength and skill sets that set us apart and allow us to thrive in different ways. Competing in a "man's world" is a silly idea, instead, change the world so both genders are playing on the same field.

As I graduated high school, I don't remember going to college thinking that men are superior than women, therefore, it never dawned on me that the gender gap would play such a huge part in my career path. I didn't realize that one day, I would have to make a tough decision in balancing work and children, I assumed that my job would be supportive. When I was in college I didn't realize that when out in the real world it was dog-eat-dog and I needed to find my voice fast or be silenced forever. I also didn't realize that some women do not advocate for other women to thrive in the workforce as they choose to be catty instead, dedicating their energy to undercut other women in the workplace instead of focusing on their own success.

I did work in college and I was ambitious and confident in where I was headed, that at one point I held three jobs while working on my master's degree. I worked at a bank since I was 18 years old; and after getting in the master's program at University of the Pacific, I held a graduate assistant position in the athletic departments media relations department. Also, in my second year pursuing my masters I held a teaching assistant position while working weekends at the bank, and then on top of that I got a job working 25 hours a week at a calendar company that worked with high profile celebrities. I did get experience and worked with several bosses with different personalities, yet I knew that those jobs were not my career path, so I didn't think about their actions with much gravity. The majority were male bosses, but my boss at the bank was female, and I still hold her dear to my heart. She truly defined "nurturing" and demanded high quality work but did so with finesse as we knew that she wanted us to succeed. The men that were my superiors at that time, however, were not nurturing, but had egos the size of a wrecking ball coming at me in full force. Although I did learn a lot from them, as you should with any boss that comes your way, I was very much intimidated by them and when I disagreed with them, I didn't feel that I could speak up.

Have a voice at a younger age and don't be afraid to speak up!

One of the many greatest things my mother taught us and I still use this as a motto in life: Be Humble: But be Confident!

This motto has always played true to who I am, so keep this in mind as we maneuver our way through a time in your life that sometimes feels confusing and difficult: Your 20s. You think you had it all figured out in college and then you get to the real world and realize, "damn, what the hell was I thinking?" You think there is something wrong, confusing, or utterly delusional about the world. The harsh reality is that we don't live with unicorns on rainbows. You ain't in Kansas anymore, the world of Oz is filled with little witches trying to keep you from achieving your goals. They are green with envy as you try to carry your red ruby slippers through the toxins of a horrible boss. However, on occasion you will be lucky to be nurtured by Glenda the good witch. It's hard, I'm not going to lie. I learned this in a very jarring way, but I am telling you how to deal with them and how you will learn not to lead others astray, so you don't have to face the same lessons I did. I do, however, want to emphasize to you that there are great leaders out there, I have had many of those as well.

There is no such thing as a difficult person, it's just that they are exhibiting behaviors that are inappropriate for the setting they are in. Even the most toxic boss is still a human trying to find their way as well; they are not horrible, they just have yet to find a way to maneuver through their behaviors properly. This type of boss also has a family and children who love them deeply, yet at work they have a hard time communicating.

The key here is communication! That was always my problem, my inability to communicate to certain bosses how they made me feel. I think that if I had, things would have been different. I always make sure to tell my staff, that if for any reason I make you feel insecure about yourself or about your work, or have offended you, please come tell me. Sometimes the stress of a job, could have a negative effect on your boss and they may take it out on you. This is why, as hard as it may be, talking to your boss about their behavior towards you will help your relationship. If their ego doesn't allow this type of criticism, at least you have done your duty.

"Honesty without tact is plain cruelty." Words can hurt, so try to always be diplomatic with your phrasing and be as respectful as possible when speaking to an authority who has caused you emotional stress. Do not address it right away, while your emotions are running high, instead take a moment to calm down and get yourself in check. It is not your job to change a person, but you can influence their behavior towards you through constructive conversation.

Working with a toxic boss or someone with authority can be emotionally draining, especially when you are new to the world of corporations, or any job really. I know what you are thinking, it's simple, I would just quit if I was faced with that type of injustice! The problem is that it is not that easy to just quit a job. I worked with a toxic boss for a few years and I stuck with it because I loved what I was doing. I loved marketing, I loved public relations, and I most definitely loved working for a shopping center. Perhaps the most important part, and the part that helped me get through the four years, was that I loved working with my peers. What girl doesn't dream of shopping and being able to work at a shopping center? For many women, myself included, it was a dream come true. The first six months of my job were great, because I was the new girl, and I believe my boss at the time thrived on having an "assistant." I put "assistant" in quotes because that is how she introduced me, even though I had a title then received a promotion. One time, she got a flat tire and had to get it fixed and I overheard her talking to her mechanic: "Yes, I'll have my assistant drop me off," like I was her chauffeur. She had me feeding her damn cats when she was away on vacation, and I HATE cats!

It wasn't that I felt I was better than anyone, but it was how she would introduce me in such a demeaning way. At that time, I had my master's degree in communication and I was only working that position to gain experience in order to further my career. When I landed that job, I felt like I was in heaven and I wanted to please my boss. I didn't want to ruffle any feathers, so in the words of Taylor Swift (I have a daughter that is obsessed with her) I would just "Shake it off."

Toxic bosses come in all shapes, sizes, genders, insecurities, or cheap pumps. The worst type of boss is when they let their insecurities play a huge role in how they manage. Notice how I use the word manage? Not LEAD. A toxic boss is never a LEADER, they know how to micromanage or just manage to make sure they look good, not you, them! They believe the world has always revolved around them, remember that when dealing with one. They especially do not know how to manage staff who are very talented and have a set of skills that they themselves lack. I do want to point out my shopping center boss's amazing qualities, as she was very optimistic, a cheerleader in the office, and the first year that I was there she thrived on teaching me and educating me about the business. I did learn many things from her, and for that I am truly grateful. Yet, I believe once I got acclimated with the job and I started getting projects from corporate, or when our leasing manager came to me and not her for information, things changed.

A toxic manager will try to suppress you and not let you move forward in your career. I was being considered for a manager role at another shopping center that our VP of Marketing had recommended. I was extremely ecstatic and up for the challenge, but at that time I had just had my daughter and was feeling stuck between what to do with my career and spending more time at home with my daughter (that is another book). I confided in my boss that if I took the job I would have to commute, since my husband's business was in our hometown and we couldn't move at that time. My other concern was my daughter and who would take care of her by the time I got home from my commute. In the Assyrian culture, it is not recommended to leave your children, especially babies, in daycare. You either have your mom, mother-in-law, or a family member that you can trust take care of children instead of placing them in a care center. I have many friends that utilize daycare when they have no other choice, but for me and my family, as well as to ease my mind when I went to work, I needed my mom or mother-in-law to take care of my daughter while I was away. I did not trust just anyone to take care of her as I would. I had visited many daycares, and I didn't care for how they took care of the babies. I remember visiting one daycare center and seeing the way the caretaker treated the babies systematically, it reminded me of the Laverne and Shirley factory scene in the opening credits (Google it if you have no clue what I am talking about). Right then and there, I decided that daycare was not for me and my family. It wasn't just my mind set, but my family would never allow me to put the kids in daycare. At that time, my mother was working the night shift at her job and my mother-in-law was working early morning shift, but they managed to take care of my daughter after they rearranged their schedules Monday through Friday so I could go to work.

My boss had taken my personal concerns and my trust in her and disclosed them to the VP of Marketing without telling me. This caused the VP of Marketing to then withdraw her recommendation and had ME call the property manager at the other shopping center and tell him that I didn't want the job. She spoke to me about how she didn't think this was a good fit any longer and how some of the issues she heard from my boss could hurt my long-term position. Am I an idiot or what?

Like a scene from "The Devil Wears Prada," I called the property manager from the other shopping center to tell him I was no longer wanting the position as the VP of Marketing stood in my office. I had no idea what had just happened! Later my property manager (who was fierce and brutally honest, and I loved it) asked the VP and my boss what had occurred. Our property manager then relayed the info to me and told me that my boss had spilled the beans when I had confided in her about my personal issues. I learned at that time, to NEVER confide any hesitations or personal issues to this particular direct boss, as she had just hurt my chances to move up the ladder.

I cautiously spoke to my boss about this as I didn't want to accuse her directly and she admitted saying something to our VP but told me it was for my benefit. I "shook it off," and I told her it was probably for the best. What I should have done was been honest about how I felt and the embarrassment and issues she caused with her office gossip. I should have told her that it was not her place to interfere with my career and talk to the VP about my concerns, that was my choice to do that, NOT HERS. I felt that she intentionally sabotaged my chance and I stood quiet, like a little sheep. I just remember the property manager from the other shopping center telling me on the phone, "Ok, but we haven't even offered you the job." Embarrassing.

With the VP making me call the property manager instead of her doing the dirty work, I realized then in that moment, just how cruel the real world works. There were other incidents before that and after that, which allowed me to change my perspective on how to deal with this certain toxic boss. It was either I got out quick or learn to manage them. The decision is ultimately up to you as you form thicker skin in the process.

There are several types of toxic bosses that you could come across in your career, and you should take the experience and learn how not to manage others or how not to be a leader. The way you are treated as you move up in your career is a stepping stone as to who you will become as a leader. You MUST take the horrible things done to you and do the opposite, *"Do unto others as you would have them do unto you,"* the Bible, Matthew 7:12, a commandment based on words of Jesus in the Sermon on the Mount.

According to Dr. Travis Bradberry in an article written for Forbes magazine titled "Six Toxic Bosses You Should Avoid Like the Plague," toxic bosses are a major drain on your energy, productivity, and happiness.

In a study from Georgetown University, 98% of people reported experiencing toxic behavior at work. The study found that toxic relationships negatively influence employees and their organizations in nine notable ways:

80% lost work time worrying about the incidents.

78% said that their commitment to the organization declined.

66% said that their performance declined.

63% lost work time avoiding the offender.

47% intentionally decreased the time spent at work.

38% intentionally decreased the quality of their work.

25% admitted to taking their frustration out on customers.

12% said that they left their job because of it.

48% intentionally decreased their work effort.

While the turnover from toxic relationships is costly, the real cost is the lost productivity and emotional distress experienced by people who are stuck in these relationships. You may know this, because perhaps you are experiencing this in your current workplace. I know this because I went through Oz thinking everyone had by back and my boss wanted me to be successful. Little did I know that my boss had little interest in seeing me promoted, at the end I felt like I was collateral damage and she wanted to get rid of me.

In an interview I conducted with Joanna Pomykala, an executive at LinkedIn, she stated that in any work environment, toxic or not, you always have to build relationships to make sure there will be people who have your back when you need help. "Find people you can trust and confide in, whether it's a colleague on your team, a friend at the company, a mentor, or someone in HR. You need a support system that you can lean on for guidance in good times and when things get tough too."

Pomykala also noted to the younger generation: "Don't complain just for the sake of complaining. Always be constructive in feedback you provide at your company, whether to your boss, a peer, HR, or even the CEO. Be aware what issues are worth shining a light on and what are not."

There are many types of toxic bosses you might come across as you stroll through the life in Oz, here are just four and how you might deal with them:

The Narcissist Boss

According to Roy Lubit in an article in the Ivey Business Journal, "Toxic managers divert people's energy from the real work of the organization, destroy morale, impair retention, and interfere with cooperation and information sharing. Their behavior, like a rock thrown into a pond, can cause ripples distorting the organization's culture and affecting people far beyond the point of impact." According to Harvard Business Review, it is easy to be fooled by a narcissist. They come across as charming, charismatic, and extremely confident, yet you later find out who they really are. Tomas Chamorro-Premuzic, the CEO of Hogan Assessment Systems, a professor of business psychology at University College London, says "they seem like the kind of person you want to work for—it's only later that you see the dark side." And the dark side isn't pretty.

When I interviewed for the job at the shopping center, I was beyond thrilled to have the opportunity to finally land a job that related to my degree. I remember the job interview like it was yesterday: the security manager was in the interview as was my future boss, she seemed so wonderful and a dream to work for. I came home to my mom and raved about her, her confidence and I how much I admired this beautiful woman and mother who was in such a dominant position at a young age. I remember complimenting her at how young she looked. The interview went extremely well and I really liked both of them. One of the things that stood out to me when she interviewed me was that she liked dressing up in different characters as she delivered invitations to the retailers for the holiday meeting before the chaos of Christmas shopping started. I remember vividly telling her that she had an exciting job and I would love to dress up with her if I had the job.

Well, I got the job and my first dress up gig was being the gorilla and she was the banana (it was a jungle theme,

I think). While walking around in the gorilla costume I saw friends walking the shopping center and I kept thinking "Thank God I'm wearing a mask." And I asked myself, *why would I tell her that I loved dressing up? Did I want the job that bad?* She did like the attention she got from guests and the managers at the retail stores, but I couldn't stand it. The worst "dress up play date" I had with her was when she made us dress up in sexy reindeer costumes, with high heels, as we pranced around the entire shopping center delivering those damn invitations to retailers. We got whistled at, we got the disgusting looks, and we had one retailer tell her "Not now, I'm with a customer, can you leave?"

Mortifying! I was beyond embarrassed and my husband was livid that I would prance around in a short mini skirt and high heels dressed as a sexy reindeer. He asked me "do you want to be taken seriously, or made fun of?" She was the show, I would just pull the wagon for her with our invites and stand there as she talked and talked and talked. Thank God for that asset of hers, as I don't like being the center of attention. At first, I thought, that this was a great thing she was doing, bringing cheer to our guests and to our retailers, and her energy was a force to be reckoned with. To me it was draining! It sucked the energy out of me and year after year of doing this I knew had to put an end to something that would extremely upset her.

According to Preston Ni in Psychology Today "Narcissists are highly averse to criticism. Negative feedback, even when reasonable and justified, threatens the narcissist's fragile sense of an idealized self, and risks triggering narcissistic injury. Common responses to criticism include anger, pretend indifference, and excuses." In addition, many narcissists are highly adept at blaming others for their own shortcomings. It's always someone else's fault.

Like I said earlier, when my daughter was born everything changed for me. It was as though there was a rebirth of the woman inside me, and I didn't tolerate my bosses slamming of doors and crying in her office (were we in 2nd grade?); or her demeaning behavior. It was Christmas time again, and this year she wanted to do a Hawaiian theme, which meant she wanted us to dress up as hula girls in coconut bras (However, I do remember she wore a shirt underneath). I loved everyone I worked with and they all were teasing me at this point because they knew I hated doing this. Our assistant property manager at the time, who was a friend and is still is one of my good friends, created a photoshop version of hula girls with my face and my boss's face on the girls. I found it to be extremely funny, but he told me that if I didn't want to do something I shouldn't have to do it, who cares if she gets mad. So, I took his advice and for the first time in three years I stood up to her and told her I was embarrassed to dress up and didn't want to do it. I told her I would come with her and pull the cart, but I wasn't comfortable dressing up as a Hula girl and walking around. She told me that I couldn't go with her, I had to dress up, or just stay in the office: so, I stayed in the office. It took a few days for her ego to calm down before she would acknowledge me, but I knew I'd done the right thing for myself.

It felt good saying no to her, but at the same time she made me feel horrible instead of being supportive of my decision. If my staff right now doesn't feel comfortable doing something, I ask them if it's OK. If they are embarrassed to do something, there is no way I would coerce them to do what they didn't want to do. That is what a narcissist does, coerce you! Our security manager told her that once, she cried, slammed her door, and didn't leave her office for a couple hours.

You can learn many things from a narcissist boss, observe how your boss makes impressions on others. Pay attention to their charisma and how they are eloquent under pressure. In addition, narcissists are often good communicators and tend to be quite visionary, the Harvard Business Review states, and also mentions that they have an ability to inspire others, and this skill can be emulated. My boss did inspire others, like I said, she had her good qualities, but her demons overshadowed her good tendencies. I remember when she organized a blood drive, which is always a great thing, but you can't coerce your staff to give blood and make them feel guilty for not doing it. I hate needles and said that I wouldn't do it, but the pressure from her felt overwhelming and she would make you feel terrible if you didn't do what she told you to do. I finally gave in to the pressure of the blood drive, and the nurse who was about to take my blood asked me several questions on the side and one of them was "Have you lived outside of the United States in the last 20 years?" I told her "Yes, I have. I lived in

Spain for five years." The nurse told me that since I had lived outside of the U.S. they couldn't take my blood. To this day I wonder if the nurse had overheard my hesitation and did me this favor to conveniently let me off the hook so my boss didn't give me a hard time. "Hey, the nurse said I couldn't give blood." And that was that.

The Harvard Business Review states that "some of the best ways to maneuver around this type of characteristic is complementing and stroking their ego. You need to figure out how to work effectively. When dealing with a narcissist, flattery will get you everywhere. They want people to love them, and they will believe any compliment you offer." I hate to say this, but pretending to admire your narcissistic boss and sucking up will generally be effective. As much as I hated doing it, I would complement her shoes, or whenever I had someone from corporate give me projects and she found out about it (and I knew she wasn't happy about me working with corporate) I would tell her that it's because I have such a great boss that I am able to take on these projects. That would put a smile on her face and she would move on and leave me alone. It was a game, and this game was about survival for me and trying to figure out how to advance in my career. I treaded very lightly and I was very careful about what I said around her, and I was always made sure to feed her ego.

However, you may be in survival mode and the saying "you have to fake it until you make it" can only be applied for so long. You must be yourself at all times and if faking it isn't working for you anymore, then you need find other options Try finding a new job and shift your career to another place that would accept you for who you are and where you can be honest with your boss about their behavior with you might be the best choice. A narcissist will always blame you for their behavior towards you, as though you have wronged them and that is the reason they are treating you gravely. The "you made me do this to you" mentality is constant in their head.

Other tendencies with a narcissist are:

They are loud.

They are arrogant.

Deceptive: *"Narcissists are often quick to judge, criticize, and ridicule. Some narcissists are emotionally abusive. By making you feel inferior, they boost their fragile ego, and feel better about themselves."* - Preston Li States in Psychology Today.

"Some people try to be tall by cutting off the heads of others." - Paramhansa Yogananda

Hypocritical: Li also states that "many narcissistic managers are unable to relate to individuals as equals. They either take an inferior position and defer to those in higher positions, or a superior position and presume that they're in some ways better than you. For them, both the superior and inferior postures are calculated to sway you to give them what they want – such is the purpose of relationships to them. They lack the empathy and humanity to treat people simply as equitable human beings."

Disingenuous: Remember when we talked about "fake it until you make it?" Well, a boss who is disingenuous looks and smells of fakeness. A smart person can read a deceitful person from a mile away and this type of boss is not only two-faced but does the opposite of what they preach. When the leaders say the "right" things but behave differently, promise the "right" things but don't deliver, commit to the "right" things but don't act on it, these behaviors create cognitive dissonance, and that creates stress among the team members which diminishes, if not destroys, morale. I remember when my boss would have guest services meeting with our guest services staff before the holidays. She would have place settings for each person with a little gift and breakfast provided. It was nice of her to do that and to take time to shop for the staff, but we all dreaded those meetings. Not because we didn't like our job, but because it didn't come across as genuine. She didn't treat us with respect and when a boss talks down to their staff, gossips, or creates hostility, then it is hard to listen and trust what they are saying when they hold meetings.

Ego: Their ego inflation is a defense against not really believing in themselves, therefore, they'll defend that over-inflated sense of self at all costs. In the words of Sarah Jessica Parker character Sarah, in the movie <u>Hocus Pocus</u>, "run amok! Amok! Amok!" So do egos running amok. Her song *"come little children, I'll take thee away, into a night of enchantment."* So, you see my little friends, narcissists can be enchanting and easily followed, but be careful as they are always out for themselves. They will suck the living life out of your good heart. Do NOT let that happen and stand up for yourself. Do not let yourself fall into that trap and lose your ethics, your values, and what is most important to you.

My husband was embarrassed that I was prancing around work half naked, and as an Assyrian wife, that is something that we do not do. I came from a strict household, and so did my husband. My husband is the most easy-going person I have ever met, but one thing that he loathes is women who do not have self-respect. He married me because I came from a good family, I was a strong woman, and I knew what I wanted. When I saw his disappointed face, I felt disgusted with myself because I knew I didn't want to do it, but I felt I had to because my boss would make me feel horrible about myself if I didn't. My mom, to this day, does not know how I was told to dress to deliver invitations. I mean, let's be honest, there was that one time we dressed in our pajamas (not sexy PJ's) but in cute pants and button up shirts (that was my favorite), but she made me hold a teddy bear the entire time (you know, to make it look like Christmas story time, teddy bears, you get it? Hey, at least we didn't wear the onesies).

Nonetheless, this experience taught me how NOT to be a leader. My staff knows what it is expected of them, and when I give them specific tasks, I ask if they are comfortable doing it. Sometimes it may be out of their comfort zone, like speaking in front of a group of people or Snapchatting with strangers at an event, but it allows them to be confident in themselves. If one of them ever came to me and said I don't feel comfortable Snapchatting or doing Live Facebooking, then I would of course give them another task. You can never make someone feel inferior to you or pressure staff to do something they do not want to do. This will kill all the morale in your office. As you move up in your career, do not let authority scare you into doing something you do not want to do: Speak UP! loud and clear.

I know that this is hard to do at times. You may think you will get discriminated towards or fired. In many work scenarios there have been sexual harassment cases that have gone on without anyone reporting them because of fear they would be to blame or higher authority would deny any accusations and create a hostile working environment.

The Insecure Boss

This is a segway from your narcissist boss to the insecure boss, because I believe that narcissists are managers who let their insecurities take over their good abilities. They are constantly wanting the attention on themselves. There is always an "I" in team with this boss. My sister's boss at a very well know social media company in the Silicon Valley is one of the best female bosses I've ever encountered, and the way my sister speaks of her is noteworthy. When my sister does a great job on a project, her boss makes sure my sister not only gets credit for it, but allows my sister to grow within the company and encourages her to work with other team managers on their projects. Her boss doesn't constrict her growth to only work with her, as long as my sister is meeting deadlines and is following up on all her tasks as her executive assistant, my sister has had the ability to assist in other areas at the social media company. In the last three years my sister has tremendously grown not only because of her very comprehensive skills and ability to take on various tasks, but also due to her boss being secure in herself to allow my sister to grow. She is constantly encouraging my sister; she allows her to be herself, she speaks highly of my sister to other VPs, and is always looking for ways for my sister to grow in the company. NOW THAT IS LEADERSHIP! My sister has been to Spain, Portugal, Chicago, Hawaii, and other various cities within the United States and worked with other departments, as they know she is reliable and has a good reputation, thanks in part to her boss's high praise.

We all have insecurities! We all have those feelings sometimes that what we are doing is not enough and believe others more successful than we are. It is normal to feel insecure. But what sets you apart from others is when you let your insecurities play a role in how you manage your staff and how you treat others at work. One of the things that is hard, is when you have been at a job for a while and someone new comes in and suddenly gets a promotion, that would kick anyone's ego down the drain. It is normal to feel jealous and frustrated as you think "what the hell is going on here?" You vent to your family or friends about this (that's OK, let it out). But one of the mistakes someone could make, is venting about it to co-workers, talking venomously about that person as you slander their name and defame their character because they received the promotion and not you. My suggestion would be to always talk to your boss in a respectful way and ask about your performance and inquire about what some of the reasons were for not getting a promotion. Being honest and upfront is the key to being successful and gaining that respect: Do NOT be the venom in the office.

In the last eight years, I have been in one job and I have had three extraordinary male bosses. They have truly shown me what a secure boss is and have supported me throughout my career. In my experience so far, these men have allowed me to grow and have given me the flexibility to take care of my family. They have been very secure in their abilities to lead and have never micromanaged me or any other staff member. It is in my opinion that my female boss at the shopping center was insecure about herself and always wanted me pressed beneath her, she always had to, in some way, make it known that she was my boss. If I got a compliment, her facial expression would change, and I would sense her jealousy. When I started working on a corporate guest services initiative with some of our VPs in the company, I knew she didn't like it. She threw out comments about how I might be taking valuable time from my current job to focus on other things. The one time she went too far was when I was leaving on my maternity leave and our one our corporate VP's sent a very nice email about how great I was doing and wished me luck with the delivery of the baby and copied my boss on it thinking I had a supportive boss. My boss in turn, copied everyone in the email and told them how she will miss me since I'm taking six months off for maternity leave.

WHAT? six months? I wish, but our maternity leave system in the United States is the second worst in the world (that's another book). Company policy was six to eight weeks of maternity leave (if you have a c-section you get eight weeks) and since I had been working at the company for more than one year, I could utilize the Family and Medical Leave Act (FMLA) that passed in 1993 for up to one year to utilize twelve-weeks of unpaid job protection. Therefore, I used an additional six weeks to get a total of twelve-weeks maternity leave, which is about three months. I was an idiot, and should have taken eighteen-weeks, but I didn't want to deal with the comments and talking behind my back that I had dealt with during my pregnancy. Her sending the email that I was taking six months off was a slighted dig about me leaving work for a long time. I remember her telling me how she worked up until she had her baby when I notified her that my doctor wanted me to leave work 2 weeks before my due date. Again, a dig and unsolicited information about her pregnancy aimed at making me feel worthless because I was taking two weeks off before having my baby. After she sent the email, I felt a punch in the gut (and it was not the baby that time).

I replied to ALL and told them that I would be back in October, which was within the next three months, with a smiley face. I went into her office and told her that I think she miscalculated the dates and the look on her face was priceless. She had nothing to say to me.

I tried so hard to never talk about my doctor appointments and the one time I took my lunch break to see my doctor, I was late from lunch because it took two hours for my doctor to see me, she loudly told me to make sure I take out the two hours from my time card.

The mistreatment of me as soon as I got pregnant was evident, but I tried not to think that it was deliberate. Much of her gossiping about me would come back to me from my colleagues.

One of the most vivid things that comes to mind is when I had just found out I was pregnant with my daughter and it was Christmas decorating time at the shopping center, and she insisted on being there until midnight to make sure the company that installed that Christmas décor did it correctly. She always brought her family to certain work events, so I assumed it was OK to bring my husband to the Christmas install, and once we were done we were going to go to my parents and tell them that I was pregnant.

My bad! She was upset that I had brought my husband and told me to just go home. Then discussed how disappointed she was in me to our property manager and couldn't believe that I had the audacity to bring my husband. I was called in to our property managers office on Monday morning and my boss was there, our property manager was very gracious about it and asked me why I had brought my husband when we were supposed to work. I told her that I assumed since my boss always brought her family, that it was OK for me to do the same. I apologized for the miscommunication and explained that I didn't mean any harm by it. My boss just sat there with her head down, not even looking at me as I spoke directly to both of my superiors. Our property manager, thank goodness, was understanding and could see that I was never told I couldn't bring family. It was partly my fault, I don't know why I assumed I could bring him since we might be there until midnight, and it was, after all, work.

The following year, I was at the install, this time with no husband. But, when I asked her if I needed to be there until midnight, she said "no, I normally don't stay that late."

The Two-Faced Boss

This is the type of boss that smiles to your face while stabbing you in the back at the same time. According to career coach Nicole Williams, author of "Girl on Top."

She told CBS News Correspondent Anthony Mason on "The Early Show on Saturday Morning" that "it's a big problem that's only getting bigger, due to the stress the economy is bringing to the workplace."

There's a difference between a tough boss and a toxic boss, Williams points out. A tough boss expects you to work hard, while a toxic boss expects you to work hard and belittles you while doing it. These days, bosses are under ever-increasing pressure and have more and more people to manage -- both of which can make a good boss into a bad one very quickly.

"Men and women are equally likely to be toxic bosses, but their techniques differ," Williams adds. "Women are more passive-aggressive, resorting to gossip and undermining, while men tend to be more overtly and aggressively toxic by using in-your-face bullying and name-calling tactics."

I have had my share of bosses, good and bad, both women and men; and I can't say that one gender is better than the other. Yet when a boss has different faces that they wear at different times, it is extremely hard to trust them. I remember bringing my daughter, who was only six months old at that time, to our work volunteer dodgeball tournament to help raise money for the homeless. My job, as always, was to bring the camera and take photos of the events. I love taking photos, so it wasn't a problem. I had my daughter in a baby sling on my chest as I took photos and stood to the side so the ball wouldn't hit us. I took a lot of photos and I was there mostly for morale support. Our property manager (PM) wanted to hold my daughter and started trying to make her walk, which she loved. I was outside talking to our assistant property manager and just really enjoying my time being there on a weekend helping a good cause.

As I stood outside, I was approached by my boss's daughter, who was probably eleven at the time, and our property manager's daughter, who was about seven years old. My boss's daughter said that her mom needed the camera and our PM's daughter then proceeded to tell me that my boss was talking about me to her mom and saying she didn't know why I was outside and not doing my job. She also told me that my boss didn't know why I would bring my baby to this event. I was furious, gave them the camera, and told our assistant PM what just happened; then I left. I came into work on Monday still upset that I was being talked about and a seven-year-old told on my boss and basically called her out. My boss came into my small office, sat on the chair and told me she knew why I was upset because our assistant PM told her, and that she never said those things. She even went as far as to tell me that sometimes children lie and make up stories. When I saw our PM I told her that my boss just called her daughter a liar, which caused our PM to defend her little girl and tell me exactly what my boss was telling her behind my back at the event to confirm that her daughter wasn't lying. I believed the seven-year-old, as children are very innocent and often tell the truth. A woman in her late 30s who was two faced, a drama queen, and manipulator, often does not.

I know I keep repeating things that happened to me at the at this specific corporate job, but that was the one experience that I invested so much of my time in and it was a good place to start my career. The calendar company job that I had when I was getting my masters, my boss was the owner, and he was a man who should have retired a long time ago. His children were basically running the business as well as his nephew, and he had a temper issue that he couldn't always control. He was a sweet man when he got his way, and sometimes he favored me over the other employees because I reported directly to him.

That job was one of the best jobs any young college student could have had. We had celebrity clients whom we published calendars for and we have secured a licensed swimsuit calendar with Playboy, again strictly swimsuit, no nudity. My job was to secure the location for the photoshoot; create a daily calendar shoot; and help choose which Playmates would be in our calendar. The location chosen was the Playboy mansion and what a fabulous location it was. My husband, whom I was dating at that time, came with me to the location shoot as well as my sister. We stayed at a great hotel off Sunset Blvd. in Hollywood and we were at the mansion for a whole week with daily breakfast and lunch provided by the mansion staff. I had an idea to create a behind-the-scenes video with a calendar purchase and while at the mansion my job was not only to make sure we were on task but that we had the appropriate people to interview for the video; I was put in charge to ask the questions along with the production team.

The memories of working at the mansion for a week and exploring the property is an experience that not many people would ever have.

We would check in daily at 8 a.m. with breakfast ready outside in mansion backyard. Some of the Playmates would be scheduled to shoot in the early morning and we were shooting in January; in their bikinis and some had photo shoots inside the infamous Grotto and in the pool. My husband's job at that time was to hold the portable heater to face the girls. Wasn't he lucky? We laugh about it now and he brags about the experience to his friends. All the Playmates were extremely nice to the staff and my other job was to plan a networking dinner opportunity with everyone involved in the photoshoot. The event was well attended after the shoot, but we never met Hugh Hefner and I never got to go inside his house as we were not allowed. I was able to attend trade-shows and in order to sell the licensed Playboy calendar and products, we also managed to secure Playmates at our booth for signings. The trade-shows were always a great fun, and I learned a lot about retail as well as branding products properly through my time at the calendar company.

The calendar job was again one of the best experiences of my life, the memories, and lessons I learned have always been a part of me, as with any job you secure. But, I quit the day my boss called me an ass. I laugh now thinking about it, even though it was verbal abuse, but it didn't emotionally bother me as much as someone who deliberately tried to not only hurt my career by slandering me behind my back, but to assassinate my character. At least my boss at the calendar company had done it to my face.

I never understood why my boss at the corporate job treated me the way she did. Especially when she would send me job openings elsewhere, so I could leave, I felt like I was a thorn in her side. On one of my days off, she made me come in with my daughter, so I could go try on clothes with the retailers for the back-to-school fashion show, none of the retailers were ready for me and didn't know I was coming. I came in to the office to see her and she told me that she didn't know why I came anyway. I told her that she told me to come in on my day off to try on the clothes; again, she made it look like it was my fault for doing what I was told to do. I don't often cry, but that day I left, sat in my car, called my husband and cried. I had to get out and get out FAST. I had finally reached my limit, and I felt like leaving was my only choice. Little did I know, that emotional abuse and things that would come out of her mouth and how she treated others as though they were the scum that live on scum, we could have reported. I was afraid, I shook it off and moved on.

One of the stories that comes to mind is a meeting with two of our sponsors at breakfast. I was telling them about my aunt and uncle whose one year old drowned in their pool because that day the gate wasn't locked. My boss had the audacity to say, "we have a pool and I would never leave a gate unlocked, I would be so careful." The ladies in the meeting just kept their head down and I felt how uncomfortable they became, but I was burning with anger inside. How dare she insinuate that my aunt and uncle were not careful? "God will only judge her one day," I thought to myself. I didn't say a word, I just sat there, furious. What was my problem? I was passive. If it had happened now, boss or no boss, I would have ripped her apart in front of the sponsors. The older you get the more you grow thick skin; and actually, be fiercer, but you don't have to wait until you get older.

My point is, be fierce now! Be fierce! Speak up for yourself, do not let someone stress you emotionally because when you bottle everything up, you will have resentment.

The Micromanaging Boss

I already feel claustrophobic talking about this and I haven't even started. According to Trish Pratt, an executive and career coach, the term micromanagement generally refers to "someone who manages a project, team or staff member using techniques that involve overly close supervision, and a lack of desire or ability to delegate tasks – especially decision-making authority." Pratt says there are varying degrees of micromanaging, ranging from a boss who needs frequent, detailed updates to one who exhibits bullying or threatening behavior. As they have typically experienced some level of success in their work, when made aware of their behavior, may defensively react in a way that says "the ends justify the means."

"From an "outside" perspective a micromanager may appear successful. Projects may get completed, schedules may be met, and results achieved. These managers are often hard workers and sometimes hold the "hard-working" standard for their group. However, from a closer perspective, it's easy to see the "fall out" that results from what some would call an "abuse of authority," is real, and can cost a company in ways they may not (or choose not to) recognize."

Pratt also suggests on her website what typical "fall out" looks like: stress. The manager using these techniques is typically stressed. More importantly, their staff members are stressed. Turnover is higher. Staff creativity and productivity are lower.

I believe that by luck our CEO's in my current job have not been micromanagers and by coincidence have been male. They never hovered over my shoulder and told me how to do my job. I believe that if they had to do my job and micromanage, then I am not doing what I was hired to do. Our newest CEO is younger than the previous two, and in the beginning had a lot of questions, but you always have to put yourself in your bosses shoes, and that is what I did with our new CEO. He was educating himself in every aspect of his duties, as he must know what each department is doing in order for him to fully function as a CEO. After putting myself in his shoes, I realized I would have done the same! I also liked that he respected us enough to ask the detailed questions that are often ignored. Sometimes he would have a different perspective on specific marketing campaigns that we probably wouldn't have thought of. I respected him for doing that and I still respect him for not only allowing us to be creative but allowing us to breathe. He, along with my previous CEOs, trusted me to get my job done and allowed for flexibility between my work and family lives. Trust is very important amongst your managers, if they do not trust you then there will be little flexibility and you will not be able to functionally do you job right.

I believe that flexibility in the workplace allows for more productive employees. Who cares where I get my deadline done, whether I work from a home computer or at the office, I am getting my job done on time. Many companies in Silicon Valley allow for this type of flexibility. My sister can work from home when needed, FaceTime in for work conferences, goes into the office for meetings, and meets all her deadlines no matter where she works from.

God, sometimes I feel like my sister and I switched lives. I always wanted the career and she always wanted the family lifestyle, yet here I am trying to make it work by having a career and making sure I am there for my children, as my husband is an entrepreneur and his work days don't allow for flexibility. Even though my husband has been magnificent in taking a couple days out of the week to take care of the kids so I can go to work, it is still exhausting. Like Sheryl Sandberg says in her book "Lean In," you must make your partner a real partner.

Well, let's get off that soap box as it is meant for another book. Sometimes there are different types of micromanagers, there are those who bully you and keep insisting on doing it their way; then there are those who are always asking where you are on the project, constantly breathing down your neck. But they mean well, they do want you to succeed, however they may be overwhelmed by demands from corporate and their success depends on your success on specific projects. With this type of boss, it's easier to talk to them, explain that you can get more work done if they let you breathe a bit without constantly asking about a task they have given you. When you have a tyrant who micromanages, that is when it is hardest to approach them about your concerns.

Remember, there is no such thing as a perfect boss. I lead a team of five employees and I still have a lot to learn about management skills and leadership roles. I do, however, know how I wouldn't want to be treated and therefore, I try to be respectful to my staff and in turn, I get that respect back from them. In my first year as director, I learned a lot about myself while making a few mistakes. I learned to always follow my intuition when hiring staff members. One of the first people we interviewed came in with an attitude and I remember him rolling his eyes at me when I gave him the written test. That was a red flag to me, but the lady I was working with at the time said he came in highly recommended and he knew everything about social media, so I hired him, and two months into the job, I knew I had made a mistake. I had to have the "I don't think this job is right for you" talk, and he said he liked it and wanted to stay, but his attitude told me otherwise.

My biggest pet peeve is when people talk behind my back and I find out about it. He and a couple of the young women I had hired said a few things, I found out, and a few days before Fair ended I told him to not return to work. After that first-year experience, I realized, you are either a County Fair person or you're not; I also realized to follow my intuition, hire humble staff members, hire people who are eager to learn, hire kind and loving people, and encourage NO DRAMA, NO TRAUMA (words from our security manager) in the office. Since then, I have hired the most fantastic team members; they are loving, kind, caring amongst each other, and I make sure there is no gossip in my office.

If there are disagreements I expect them to work it out or talk to me if they disagree with me. It's been eight years since my first year as a manager and I have learned a lot about myself, but most importantly my office is open to my staff to talk to me about any discrepancies. If, for some reason, I have said something to hurt someone's feelings or have miscommunicated something, I make sure that they feel comfortable enough to talk to me about it, because it was probably a misunderstanding. I have my staff's best interest at heart and I feel like they are my children at times. I want them to be successful, I want them to move on to better things, to use their experience with me and to land that perfect job they are striving for. I am their advocate and their mentor, and over the last eight years I have kept in touch with the majority of my former staff and they come visit me in the office during the Country Fair. I love knowing that I have a little something to do with my little network of former employees' success in their careers.

I have learned from some of my managers how NOT to lead others, and from other managers I have learned how to lead. The experience I have had with toxic bosses lead me to be the type of leader I am today. I know in my heart I truly care for my staff and want the best for them, and at the same time I do ask that they do their job and seek to manage their projects. I do not manipulate my staff, I do not coerce them, and I certainly do not talk about them behind their backs. They are the ones that make me successful, they make my department look good, therefore, with confidence I can say that I must respect and act in a way that earns that respect back from them. I have learned to be a tough person and have thick skin, so when I do not agree with something I make sure my voice is heard, but I do it with tact.

Some of our older Assyrian women are extremely fierce and would never let anyone walk all over them. The majority of these older women rule with an iron fist; the fist that has gone through years of raising children, rolling dolma, and cleaning the house, yet they know more about leadership than any one of us that have gone to college.

My husband's grandmother (Nana Meggie) is a fierce woman and she always says that if she was born and raised in the United States, she "would have captured the world by her hands." The translation gets lost from Assyrian to English, but what she means is that women born and raised in this country must be able to take control of their destiny and they can capture anything they want. Nana Meggie was born in Urmia, Iran, and came from a poor household, and as Christians they were the minority in the country. After she married, they moved to Baghdad, Iraq for a while and then moved back to Iran. Once the Shah of Iran, Mohammad Reza Pahlavi, was overthrown because of the revolution in February of 1979, Nana Meggie and the rest of their family fled to various European countries in the 1980s and finally settled in the United States in the early 1990s. My mother-in-law tells me the stories of how they escaped Iran with my husband and my sister-in-law. It was 1985 and the new Iranian regime, by the new President Khomeini, had taken over, which brought many changes to the Christians in Iran and the rest of the citizens as well. Gone were the freedoms under the Shah and the citizens quickly faced oppression.

My mother-in-law tells me how her and my father-in-law walked with their two children to Turkey, with each security check facing a death sentence. From Iran, they had to cross a river in the middle of the night, and one of the youngest passengers on the boat was a baby who was crying loudly, and as guards stood by in the bushes near the river and the boat reached a point where it was going past the guards, everyone was trying to hush the baby. By the Grace of God and Prayers, the baby suddenly stopped crying as the boat quietly went past the guards. My husband was only five years old at the time but remembers it vividly, especially when they reached a security checkpoint to get to Turkey. That moment was one of the scariest, as they took my father-in-law to be questioned, he faced death or going back to Iran, which meant death for the entire family since they had also escaped. The officer interrogating my father-in-law (Eddo) held him in a room for hours, and finally brought his high-ranking officer to speak with my him. As soon as he saw my Eddo, this particular high ranking Iranian officer remembered him from their younger years when they shared a bunk in military school. He hugged Eddo and told him he was going to let them go, gave them back all their paperwork and even asked one of his officers to take them where they needed to go in Turkey. Again, by the Grace of God, my in laws were free and were able to travel to Greece afterwards to stay with my husband's aunt for the next five years.

In that desperation, in the moments faced with death with two young children in her arms, how did my mother-in-law face adversity? She tells me how terrified she was and how cold the children felt, but didn't utter a word. They were hungry for days and thirsty to only wanting to escape the regime of Iran at that time. I ask myself, how did they leave all their belongings, albums, family, and their parents behind to start a new life? I'm not sure my children now would be able to survive such hardships, or maybe when faced with cruelty you have no choice.

My father faced similar hardship at only 18 years old. My family came from Baghdad, Iraq and he was forced to leave his country at a young age so that he wouldn't have to join the military. As soon as you turned 18 years old, men in Iraq had no choice but to be accepted to University or join the military. My father left his country, his parents, his friends, his home, and travelled to a country he knew nothing about. He lived in Canada with his sister for a few years and was overwhelmed by depression and homesickness.

I tell you these stories because my family has faced many obstacles to get to a place where we felt safe, so their children can live a happier life with more opportunities. Therefore, when I am faced with adversity, I think of them and what they endured. They fought to get here, and I must make something of myself for them. My passive demeanor, overtime, has turned into being more courageous while facing difficult people head on. Maybe it takes years in a career and ability to form courage, but I am telling you that if something occurs and you feel like you are being verbally abused, taken advantage of, or disrespected, you must not "Shake It Off." You Must speak up! Once someone does something to you and gets away with it because you shook the incident off, they will do it repeatedly. If speaking up doesn't do anything, then write down and document the incidents and make sure human resources is aware of what is occurring.

Oh Mother!

I know, I know what you are thinking. This is going to be the boring chapter where I tell you the boring things about human resources or HR. But if you, like me at your age, do not understand your rights and what resources are available to you, you will regret it. You must understand the importance of the human resource department as they do not just help you fill out your employee paperwork, but they are there as a resource should you ever feel discriminated against, are being harassed, verbally abused at work, have a hostile work environment, or your manager is not allowing you to take the allowed time off. It could be several things, but most importantly you must read your company policies as each state has different sets of HR policies that the company must abide by.

I never, in my career, had the guts to write formal complaints about my bosses, even though at the shopping center I should have for emotional abuse. But, even then I didn't want to create a hostile working environment for myself, and my passive character didn't think that what I was experiencing was anything out of the norm. Little did I know that a boss should never treat their employees the way I, and others I worked with, were treated. I mean, what would HR do for me anyway? The company did issue out a hotline for employees to call should they feel discriminated against or feel they were mistreated, and the call would be anonymous. I was afraid to speak up and ruffle feathers! Actually, in all honesty, it never crossed my mind to complain to HR or my boss's VP. I thought, if I did complain, I would be fired or put in a position where she would treat me extremely unkindly.

The only time I dealt with HR was when I was doing my paperwork for my maternity leave when I was about to have my daughter. It was information that I researched and talked to HR a lot about because I wanted to make sure I was taking the allotted time off. Again, I took 12-weeks off for maternity leave, plus the two weeks that my doctor told me to stay home before I had my daughter. During my 8th month of pregnancy both my property manager and my boss asked me to come to my boss's office for a talk. They asked that I closed the door behind me and my stomach was in knots. *"What the heck do they have to tell me now?"* I asked myself. I could tell they had teamed up to talk to me about this and it was something my boss had probably complained about. I didn't sit, I remained standing and waited. My property manager was leaning against my boss's table and said they wanted to know "if I was sure I was allowed to take the 12 weeks for my maternity leave." "Are you sure you can take that much time off?" "Also, I worked all the way up until I had my baby and are you sure you can leave two weeks before your due date." Are you kidding me? I respected my property manager, but I couldn't believe what was coming out her mouth as my boss sat in her chair just staring. Really? You are going to ask me these questions NOW when I'm about to go on maternity leave?

I told them that I had been in contact with HR for months, filled out my paperwork, and that corporate has all my information. "I have filled out my Family Medical Leave Act (FMLA) for the extra six weeks off and job protection." They both stared at each other as though they had concluded that they couldn't do much about it. I walked back to my office and felt horrible for taking that much time off *"Do I have the right to do that?"* I wondered. I called corporate to make sure I had done everything correctly, and HR assured me that I had and I should enjoy my time off with the new baby (at least they made me feel good).

Looking back now, my property manager and my boss had no right to interrogate me like that, especially being eight months pregnant and making me feel horrible for taking the allotted time off for having a baby. Also, no one should make you feel guilty for taking two weeks off before having a baby. Before I left on maternity leave, I remember telling my boss that if she needed me to do anything during my time off to let me know. *"I can work from home."* Jeez what a concept, which back then was looked at as a taboo. She told me I couldn't work from home since I was on disability, the company would not allow it, but I felt like I had to offer something since I was made to feel so guilty for taking that time off.

Well, guess what happened a year later? Both of my bosses got pregnant. Guess who took the entire 12 weeks for maternity leave? Both!

If I knew what I know now, I would have most certainly complained about the hostility I felt when going on maternity leave. I would have filed a formal complaint to HR about the treatment and documented every single conversation; everything said to make me feel like a worthless employee. When you become pregnant, know your company rules and understand the FMLA and maternity leave laws. Knowing those will save you stress when dealing with potentially difficult management.

My former boss, who was a man, at my current job told me after having my third baby, "Adrenna, the work will be here when you leave and when you get back. Take as much time as you need with your baby and don't worry about work." He made me feel important, he didn't make me feel guilty for having a baby, and he wanted me to take care of myself first. He never bothered me in the months I took off, and when I was ready to come back, which was 18 weeks later, he welcomed me enthusiastically and said, "I missed you, hope you are doing well."

I do have to say though, I did get that same welcome back at the shopping center. My boss told me to go visit my daughter for lunch and she did buy my daughter pink Vans shoes. It was sweet of her! I'm not sure if she truly missed me or she was just happy to have her "assistant" back. Nonetheless, I enjoyed the moments when my boss was nice and not conniving.

Maternity leave in the United States is the second worst in the world and according to an article in Forbes magazine titled "U.S. Dead Last Among Developed Countries When It Comes To Paid Maternity Leave" by Rita Rubin, researchers published a study for the Centers for Disease Control and Prevention, which analyzed national survey data: Employed women who received 12 weeks or more of paid maternity leave were more likely to start breastfeeding their baby and continue to breastfeed for at least six months, as recommended by the American Academy of Pediatrics, than women who did not get any paid leave.

In an article by Rita Rubin in Forbes Magazine, she states that women who had fewer than 12 weeks of maternity leave and fewer than eight weeks of paid leave were more likely to have more symptoms of depression. "The mother's mental and physical health can be an important route through which infants are affected by parents' employment decisions."

According to Rubin, the 1993 Family Medical Leave Act (FMLA) provides 12 weeks of unpaid leave, but you have to work for a company with at least 50 employees or a public agency or public or private elementary or secondary school to qualify. Plus, you have to have worked at least a year for your employer, racking up a minimum of 1,250 hours.

More than 40% of U.S. workers do not meet all of the FMLA requirements, and even if they do, many can't afford to take unpaid leave. Only 12% of U.S. workers in the private sector can get paid family leave through their employer, according to the Department of Labor. Some of the rest have even turned to crowdfunding websites to raise money for maternity leave.

Pomykala stated in our interview that "there is never a perfect time to start a family, there will always be trade-offs when balancing a career and having children. And you can take steps to make this an easier transition. While the US is still far behind other countries with its parental leave policies, there are many companies that have made big strides ensuring that new mothers and fathers are given the time away from work and support they need when they start new families. There are many resources available to research companies who offer great maternity and parental leave policies to their employees."

In 2017, President Trump signed a bill that allowed new mothers who are not given maternity leave by an employer to be paid six weeks of unemployment benefits by the government. According to an article in The Independent by Charlotte England, the President said he crafted the policy with the help of his daughter Ivanka Trump. However, it still only equates to just 2.8 weeks on an average salary, placing the US at the bottom in comparison to 14 other countries.

I have had many female friends in situations not knowing what to do after having a baby. Do they stay home? Do they go back to work full time? Will work allow them to have a flexible schedule? Maybe they can be part time? I wonder if having a gap in my resume or if I say I was a "stay at home mom" will be sufficient enough when I go back to work? I have friends now who have their education and are extremely skilled women who chose to stay home with their children because that is what worked for their family dynamic. I also have friends who thrive and are better moms when they work full time. They will find that being at home all day with the kids or running errands is not for them and they need the adult interaction to feel fulfilled. Then there are moms like me, who chose to work somewhere between part time and full-time and be home with my children. I teach at our community college and my current position at the County Fair allows me to make my own hours, which is great.

I can fulfill my need to work and make a difference as well as being there for my kids. I pick them up from school; I help in their classroom; I drop them off at the sports or other activities and much more. That was important to me and my family. As you become engulfed in this thing called Motherhood, you will have to make specific choices that you never thought you would need to, but, remember to always do what is best for you family needs and what is best for you. If you feel that you need to be a stay-at-home mother, then stay home. No one needs to judge you because of it or encourage a stigma that you "are not doing anything" or "what does she do all day." Dammit I'm with my darn kids all day, keeping them busy, cooking, doing laundry, cleaning, picking up and dropping them off at activities! No one has the right to judge you. Now, if you choose to be a full time working mom, that is just as wonderful. The stigma of "you have someone else raising your kids," or "she doesn't see her kids at all," has no truth. You are raising your children and your children are watching their mom be a leader in the workforce. Do not let stereotypes make you feel guilty. Although, it is normal to feel guilty when you start working after having your children.

I remember feeling extremely guilty when I first went back to work after having my first child. I thought about what she was eating; when was she sleeping? Was she happy? Does she know that mom loves her even if I am away? Even though my daughter was with my mom or my mother-in-law and I knew she was in extremely good hands, I still felt guilty. They would send me photos of her and when I would pick her up they would tell me of the milestones that she had achieved that day and I just couldn't take the fact that I wasn't there for her accomplishments. I remember walking in to my parents' house when my daughter was nine months old and my mom excitedly telling me that my daughter had taken her first steps (very early for a baby but my daughter did a lot of things early, now my boys are a different story...), I just smiled and didn't want to show to my mom that I was disappointed that it didn't happen with me around. After that, I made a conscious effort to start looking for a job that not only cared about me as a person but something flexible that allowed me to be there for those milestones with my kids.

The Pew Research Center reported that after three decades of decline, the percentage of stay-at-home mothers is rising. According to World Bank, the female labor participation rate dropped 59 percent in 2000 to 56.3 percent in 2014. Childcare costs are extremely high and sometimes it makes it difficult to work and afford for childcare. Some women are staying home because it makes more sense financially than paying for childcare. One of my friend who works full time, pays over $2,300 a month for child care! She loves the daycare because they are warm and friendly with her children, but the price they pay for that nurturing environment is forcing her to now look for cheaper options. Yet, she doesn't want to sacrifice her children's wellbeing for a lower cost option. She feels stuck! She confides in me that sometimes she tells her husband that they should have saved up for child care way before having kids. Childcare has become a financial and emotional burden on parents and companies in the United States must do a better job at providing better options for moms if they want to retain them in the workforce.

So, what if moms start staying home more? That is their choice, right? Yes, but companies are losing out on diversity of thought and innovative creativity. What can companies do to keep these moms at work? My suggestion would be to provide a more flexible work scenario for new parents. The notion of staying every day in the office from 8am-5pm is slowly transitioning to a more flexible work schedule, especially for those working in the tech world. My sister is an executive assistant and knows not to book any meetings for her boss before 9 am or after 3 pm. Her female boss shares the responsibility with her husband to drop off and pick up their kids from school and to take them to their extracurricular activities.

For women who are coming into the workforce right after having a baby there should also be a transition period once back to work to help moms adjust to the new change. Some companies have a policy called the "phase back to work" scheduling where new moms work 50 percent of the time and the following week will work 75 percent and then transition back to their full-time hours. This helps alleviate any anxiety leaving your newborn with a proper nanny or daycare. Companies must first build trust in their employees in order to cultivate engaged employees. Employers who trust that you will get the work done will likely not bat an eye when you leave early to pick up your children.

According to a recent study done by Dr. Ruth Tubey, Kipkemboi Jacob Rotich; and Dr. Alice Kurga titled History, Evolution and Development of Human Resource Management: A Contemporary Perspective, they explain that HR is a product of the human relations movement of the early 20th century, "when researchers began documenting ways of creating business value through the strategic management of the workforce. The function was initially dominated by transactional work, such as payroll and benefits administration, but due to globalization, company consolidation, technological advancement, and further research, HR now focuses on strategic initiatives like mergers and acquisitions, talent management, succession planning, industrial and labor relations, ethical considerations, diversity and inclusion. These, among other initiatives contribute to the understanding of Human Resource Management as a contemporary issue owing to their sustained evolutionary nature."

Companies in the United States are still new compared to their European counterparts, who have more established HR processes. Yet, U.S. companies have always led the way we manage, however, we should take some lessons in how to balance work and life. Silicon Valley's tech companies, such as Yahoo!, Google, Facebook, LinkedIn and Netflix are leading the new way of managing and retaining working moms. They have opted to help make childcare more affordable through subsidies and have created a more flexible working life.

One of my really good friends whom I have known for over 17 years now works for a very prominent company in Silicon Valley and had a really hard time transitioning back to work after having her baby. She battled postpartum depression for over a year and struggled to be fully present at work. She wasn't getting along with her boss, which made things worse for her and as much as she wanted to quit several times, she didn't have the support she needed to stay home. They needed the money, and she was working for the health benefits the job offered. One of the frustrating things for her was not knowing whether staying at home would benefit her emotionally, or if staying at a job she didn't like anymore would help fill the void of her postpartum depression. I remember telling her to speak to her HR department about her ill treatment from her boss, but that was out of the question, as she said speaking with HR would create a more hostile working environment from her boss knowing that the complaint came from her. I thought, well what is HR there for? Aren't they supposed to help in these situations? She answered yes, but they most likely would side with her boss and then my job would be in jeopardy. I did tell her of the situation when my mom went to her HR to complain about misconduct with one of her supervisors, she was not afraid to put the complaint in even though her boss knew it was coming her, and he became a lot more professional when dealing with my mom knowing that HR was investigating him. I'm sure he resented my mom for complaining and creating more chaos, but for my mom it was more about being treated with respect than it was worrying about his feelings concerning HR.

As you start working in the real world after college, you will soon realize that each company has its own set of policies that you need to educate yourself on. The current company I work for doesn't have an HR department, we must work directly through the State, which makes it harder. We do have board members that we can file complaints to if needed, but for the most part we have learned to handle difficult situations on our own as a work family. Our CEO has created a flexible work environment that allows me to be home with the kids when needed and if situations arise amongst colleagues, we know we can speak to him without it jeopardizing our job.

Good, hard working people stay in jobs because of good employers. Some good hard-working people love their job but have toxic bosses who then leave the company. However, with a knowledge of proper HR channels, the employees who work under vile bosses may be able to do something about it. A good boss leads, a horrible boss manages. Don't be a manager! Be a leader! Be empowering!

Be Empowered

In the summer after I turned 5 years old, we moved to Vitoria, Spain. This was a turning point in my young life as this was the time I would experience the world outside of what I was used to. I remember crying terribly in the airport as my mom peeled me out my grandmother's arms, as I didn't want to let her go. My grandmother had taken care of me for the first two years of my life and she was my world. I don't quite remember when we entered the beautiful country of Spain, the ride to our new apartment complex, or carrying any suitcases. I just remember feeling lonely in a place that was unfamiliar, and worse I didn't know the language.

It was just my sister, my parents, and I who only spoke Assyrian and English. The reason we had moved to Spain is because my father started managing a steel company in Vitoria, Spain. The owners of the company were from Kuwait, and my uncle, my dad's brother, helped manage a company as well. So, here we were, in the middle of summer with no family, no friends, not even a pet; the only things we had were pictures, our blankies that we carried with us, and some of our toys.

We situated ourselves in a three-bedroom apartment on a quiet street in Vitoria. Across from us was a park with cement ground, and one time my sister and I were playing on the merry-go-round and she went flying onto the cement, hitting her head so hard that we had to take her to the doctor's office. She had a huge cone head for a week, but in the end, everything was fine. Across from us was also a small grocery store, a bakery, a salon (which is where my mom would end up as one of their best clients), a pharmacy, a candy store (which we children became regulars at), and a bike shop. My mom enrolled me at Sagrado Corazon (pronounced Corathon, with the TH), the translation in English is Sacred Heart, elementary school.

I caught on rather quickly to the customs while in school and my fondest memories at that school were the nuns playing jump rope with us. I vividly remember crying for my mom and one of the nuns picked me up, put me on her lap, and in Spanish telling me it was going to be ok. I remember her face as, of course, the nuns wore the traditional nun veil. She was older, with glasses, but had kindness in her voice to put me at ease. Although the nuns were kind, they were stern and we all knew to respect them as well as obey any of their commands.

Sagrado Corazon taught me Spanish and the Spanish culture, within months I was speaking Spanish like a native and translating Spanish for my parents. I was later moved to a boarding school in Vitoria called Izarra. I was never in the housing units, but the bus would pick my sister and me up close to our house and drop us off at school. We would leave school at 5pm and by 6pm we were home. I truly loved my experience as a kid there and met so many friends from various parts of the country. My friend Landi was British and her mom was one of our English teachers. They lived on campus in the housing units, which we would sometimes go to during our 90-minute lunch breaks (WOW, this is unheard of in the U.S. schools). At that school and living in Spain I learned how to adapt well to the ever-changing world around me. The kids in Spain were kinder, wise beyond their years, but had the same issues of teasing or 7-year-old girl drama. I was well liked in my class because I came from The United States and we all loved Madonna as she was very popular in the 1980s. My friends, Sarah,

Landi, Marta and Tatiana and I would sit under a table singing "Papa Don't Preach."

We had a small car and sometimes my dad would take us to France and we would visit Lourdes, France where the Virgin Mary appeared to St. Bernadette. We traveled to Baghdad, Iraq where my parents grew up and we would visit my uncle and his family in Kuwait. I would say by the time I was 9 years old I was able to speak Assyrian, English, Spanish, understood Arabic and was learning French. Children in Europe are not only more culturally well rounded, but the vast array of languages they have the potential to learn is astonishing. I received very good grades with great math scores, which boosted my confidence in school. Spain was our home and after years of living there we made friends, who became our family, attended weekly mass at the Catholic church by our house and I didn't have to translate for my parents any longer. By 1986, my parents welcomed their third child, my little brother Emmanuel.

My mom actually went to the U.S. to have him so he could be a citizen right a way without dealing with immigration forms when we moved back to the U.S. I remember leaving my school and friends in the middle of the semester because my mom had to be about 7 months pregnant or less to be allowed to travel. My parents temporarily put us at an elementary school in California where we lived my grandmother. As happy as I was living with Nana again, I was not a happy camper at that school. I was made fun of because of my thick English accent in California, and I remember being bullied in the playground by a young boy with curly blonde hair as he would always try to push me down the slide. One time, he pushed me so hard that I scraped my knee on the gravel. That was my first incident as a child with bullying or harassment and I never spoke up, never told the teacher, never told my parents; I just took it and never said anything to anyone or to him.

I adjusted well for the temporary three months, did my homework, did my classwork, and the best part was my Nana picking me, because she would be waiting for me by the fence with a huge grin on her face ready for a hug. There is nothing more precious to me than a grandmother's love and our talks were always about all the things my parents wouldn't let me do, like eat ice cream before dinner. Then we all went back to Spain, and the relief was overwhelming as I had missed my school and friends. I was back in the groove with the Spaniards and I was extremely happy to be at a place that I cared for. Our teachers there were very well respected, and I do remember being hit on the bottom for talking in class, but I never did it again.

Although I loved being in Spain, the longing to be with family started to weigh heavily on my parents and us children as well. When my dad's Steel company shut down, we were moved back to the U.S. and lived close to my grandparents. We were happy that the family was back together, and my mom was pregnant with her fourth child, my little crazy brother, and Adam was born in 1988.

My parents enrolled my sister and I at a private Catholic school in the city we lived in. I have fond memories at this school, as it was a great school, but I became the classic story of the Ugly Duckling in the life. I had to wear glasses, and not just normal glasses, thick plastic light pink glasses with old lady string hanging so they wouldn't fall on the ground. I then got braces in 6th grade which was the worst look for any 12-year-old girl. I was made fun of, being called four eyes and I know kids were talking behind my back.

I wasn't the cool kid anymore, as I was in Spain. I was the foreigner who was put in English as a Second Language (ESL) courses, which made me fall behind in math class, and I was no longer good in math class as I had been in Spain. All those issues played into my confidence and I didn't feel like I was smart enough, cool enough, or anything at all. My mom was always good about making sure that we always had a positive image of ourselves, so when kids made fun of me, I always brushed it off. I remember in 8th grade running for office and my dad helping me with my speech. I wasn't the cool kid to be running for office, what was I thinking? Why did I put myself through kids saying "you can never win," and why would I let my dad help me with the speech. He told me to say, "God Bless you all and God bless this school" at the end of my speech. Jesus Christ, I could still hear the snickering. I was never depressed about it, or ever made to feel less worthy than them. But, it did hurt my feelings and I never said anything back to these kids. I, again, would just let it go.

My insecurities started growing as I got into my teenage years, and to make it worse, our parents had moved us to another school again. All of my friends from the Catholic school I had attended with were going to a Catholic High School, and my parents decided to enroll me in a public high school.

Oh my, did my eyes open up to that. I thought there were only Catholics in the world I came from, but once I entered the public-school system I met all types of religions. I remember high school freshman orientation being dreadful, as I didn't know anyone. I felt alone again as I had at 5 years old in Spain, in a new world, but this time I spoke the same language as them. I was once again the ONLY Assyrian, and no one in that school knew what or who Assyrians were as I was in the cowboy capital of the world and the majority of students were white and Hispanic.

I did meet a Middle Eastern girl at the orientation who started introducing me around and she seemed to know everyone (she ended up becoming our school president our senior year). She knew I was new and who I was right away and asked me what nationality I was. She spoke

Arabic to me but I didn't know how to speak Arabic, only Assyrian. We became friends, but not as close since she was integrated with the more popular crowd and I was an outsider.

Freshman year was a tough year, as I made the volleyball team without trying out and this put me in an awkward position. I remember coming to practice in my regular clothes, no gym clothes, and playing with girls who had to go through tryouts and conditioning. I was oblivious to this and didn't know why they were so rude to me. I remember pumping the ball back and forth with three of the girls. All three girls already had a friendship formed from elementary school and here I was making the team, and I wasn't even that good. I could feel their anger and their attitude as none of them wanted to be my partner or talk to me. That was 24 years ago, and one of the girls and I are now best friends, and I also keep in touch with the other two. We four formed a bond through the game of volleyball in our four years together in high school, as they eventually got over their anger in the weeks following the start of our Freshman year and we quickly became friends.

Giving people chances and getting to truly know them is how we will get through obstacles at work or any adversity with colleagues. We look back at our 14-year-old selves and laugh now at how I was treated, and they always apologize when we bring the subject up. I laugh at it as well, and tell them how "bitchy" they were, but the end is what matters. I have shared 24 years of life experiences with my one true best friend, and I wouldn't trade how we met for anything.

Just like any new person that comes into a new job, we scrutinize that person, talk about them, and some colleagues do not give that person a chance to show their true personality and gifts. We must empower others before we feel empowered in our job and in your personal life. Get to know that "new" person, see where they come from? What experiences have they had? Have them start talking about themselves and see the type of connection you could make with this person. Empowering others has always made me feel empowered in myself, because I have never been a selfish person and listening is key to forming relationships.

Listening is empowering!

In teaching speech communication, one of the first lessons in my curriculum is listening skills. I tell my students the importance of truly listening to what someone is saying before rushing to conclusions about their message. Here is what I tell my students:

Three causes of not listening:

Not concentrating

Listening too hard

Focusing on delivery and personal appearance

Four ways to become a better listener:

Take listening seriously

Resist distractions

Don't be diverted by appearance or delivery

Suspend judgment

Always have an open mind, it will make a difference in how we judge others. We will not always get along with everyone, or agree with opinions, but as long as we treat each other with respect and be honest to that person in how we feel, that is the key to being a successful employee. There will be problems at work and we will sometimes not see eye-to-eye with someone, but it is always best to talk directly to that person instead of behind their back. The number one rule I have in my office with my staff, is not to talk about each other.

Once the office becomes toxic, it is hard to manage, and it becomes an unhealthy work environment. It happened to me in my previous job and I saw how toxic it was to work in an office full of nonsensical drama. My motto at work and with my staff is "Just do your job and go home." Very simple, right? Why get involved in another department's drama? Why get involved in the gossip at work? Knock on wood, my office over the last eight years, excluding the first year I was there, has been drama free and I love it that way. It is peaceful when I come home, and if I have issues with my staff or see that they have slacked off, I tell them. There is a sense of ownership I instill in them to make sure they know that they must manage their own projects; if I end up having to do their job, we will have a problem.

My first year as the marketing director at this new job was not easy. It was actually quite hard and I learned many lessons about myself thanks to the experience. I was new to the job and was not trained at all; I was given a binder to read over Christmas break in December of 2009 and I remember reading the binder and feeling insecure about not being able to do the job properly. What I did know is that I loved public relations, marketing, handling guest relations issues, and media relations. What I was scared of was the unknown of the jobs magnitude and media relations during a crisis.

The first day on the job I needed to start hiring people and my mistake was going through the pile of people who had originally applied for my position and didn't get the job. It was a mistake because most were eager for my job and for some reason were not chosen for that position, therefore, if I would hire one from that pile they would try to prove that they should have been the right choice by undermining every decision I made. I also hired someone who had applied for my job (big mistake), and then I hired a project manager who had previously worked with me at another job.

I always tell people, you are either a County Fair person, or you are not. There is no in between! Well, the three hired were not Country Fair people. Two months into the job, the eye rolls from the social media coordinator got worse and the talking behind my back increased with the other two that I hired. I, of course, sat with all of them and talked to them about what the issues were, and they couldn't really tell me exactly what it was. The social media coordinator was extremely disrespectful to me and when I called him out and sent an email to my CEO about his behavior, all three would go to lunch and come back with attitudes. The worst part for me was taking a chance on my friend who had previously worked with me. She knew my personality and who I was and said "I think there is a power struggle." I don't ever use the "I am the BOSS" card.

Respect as a leader should NEVER be demanded. It is earned from your staff! Yet, if one employee is being disrespectful, talks behind your back, and isn't forward or honest about why they are feeling that way, then there are repercussions for that employee. You have to seek proper channels with HR by documenting everything with that employee and your interactions with them. Since we didn't have an HR department, I took everything to my CEO! From emails sent; to meeting with the group; to all the verbal communication I had with all three, he saw my evidence and told me to take any necessary action I needed with his full support. Therefore, my decision was to release them of their duties immediately after the fair was over.

Looking back, I learned a valuable lesson! I should have never hired staff immediately without me knowing what my own job entailed. I hired staff that I needed to train, when I didn't even know what I was doing in my job and had my own insecurities about it. I think it showed, and the staff thought I didn't know what I was doing and didn't respect my authority. Another lesson learned was not listening to my intuition and not doing things to appease people. I have always been a people pleaser, but after being a director, you realize you cannot please everyone. You must do what is best for you and best for the company, or you will falter in the future. After my first year as marketing director of the fair, I hired the staff that I really felt comfortable hiring and since then I have had the joy of seeing over 30 staff members grow in their career, work for companies such as Disney and Gallo Winery, become professors in Los Angeles, work at newspapers, and one has been by my side as she worked towards her law degree for the last seven years. I keep in touch with former employees and I am there for them as much as I am there for my students whenever they need anything.

I worried after my first year at the County Fair that I wasn't going to be a good manager, but I learned to be a good leader and I am still learning to this day. I learn daily from my staff, I learn from my students, I learn from my colleagues, and I listen. My tech guy and I have a lot of differences, I tell him he reminds me of the Jimmy Fallon, Saturday Night Live character "The Computer Guy." We've had our share of conflict but listening to him speak about his upbringing one day and him saying "I know I turn people off because I am so short with people," I have learned to understand where he comes from, and try to really work with his personality. We are all different, yet we must learn to work with each other. He is a human just like me and sometimes even if we don't see eye-to-eye, I must do a better job in communicating, I mean, it is in my job title after all.

Our experiences undoubtedly shape who we are. My experience at the shopping center could have easily transformed me into someone I hated just to make it in the real world and climb that ladder. Pay attention to who you really are and be yourself. Be aware of the traits and what you disliked of former employers because you can use the opposite in your own leadership role as you progress in your career. Sheryl Sandberg states in her book Lean In, it's a "Jungle Gym, Not a Ladder." You can either let your negative experiences devour you and make you a hollow person, or you take those experiences, those insecurities and become a powerful leader in anything you do. Be the opposite of what you disliked about any former employer. Learn to channel your positive skills and turn any negative experience into a positive world for your team and colleagues.

I want to stress to never change who you are in the workplace. Never think that you have to be one person at work and another person in your personal life. Be empowering to yourself at an early age because as you get older, you will understand that that is key to success. Just be You! If you feel that your employer does not like your personality or they make comments about your personal life and who you are on the inside, then that is not the right job and place to be at. If it IS the right job to be at, then seek the proper channels through HR to help correct the problems.

Currently, my staff is very diverse in personalities. I have my quiet marketing coordinator who doesn't utter a word but is extremely smart and does her job very well. I have my sassy project manager, who has been with me for seven years and is studying to be a lawyer, she tells it like it is and will normally put anyone in their place if they are wrong. I have my social media coordinator, who is quiet, but has a dry sense of humor and makes us laugh uncontrollably and has an innocent heart. My sponsorship coordinator is very talkative, loud, expressive, yet a humble, kind and beautiful soul. I wouldn't have it any other way, and when I hire, I hire for their attitude more so than their qualifications, it is important that they are fit to do the job, but attitude is top priority. I can train someone to do their job, but I can never train someone to change who they are. I hire people that will fit within my team and be a team player.

My team is also full of Millennials! In my experience here is what I have observed so far from them so far... They work hard, manage their projects, and have the same drive to make it in the world that I did at their age. They also tend to be very tech savvy, which is excellent, and they strive for a work/life balance, which is very dear to me as I remember my struggle when having children and working. These Millennials, though, know that they want it now! And why not? The generation before me was always ruthless in clocking in at exactly 8am and clocking out at exactly 5pm. My generation, which I like to call the Xennials, are in between Generation X and the Millennials, and tend to see the value of balance. You do not have to clock in at exactly 8am. Depending on the job and your position you must respect the hours given to you, for example if your employer tells you the job requires you be here from 8am until 5pm, you must respect the hours and be there on time. You must have the conversation with your employer if you need have a flexible schedule, and if your position allows for flexibility. If you are a receptionist and you are required to open at 8am and you consistently show up late, you will have a problem. There are positions that allow flexibility and if that is what you are seeking then you must tell your employer and work out the schedules ahead of time. It's not just about the employee, but about the company and the brand you represent. If you are motivated with a flexible schedule and you still get your job done and probably will give your employer your best work because of the flexibility given. Who would have thought flexible schedules could be so useful?

One of the skills I have learned over the years is that speaking up is an essential skill to really developing respect and making sure you don't take any emotional baggage home with you. Especially after having kids, I have learned that when I take any conflict home with me that I haven't resolved during the day, I become an irritable mother. I am impatient with my children, I can't stop thinking about my work interaction, and I feel anxious all day and night until it is resolved. It is not my children's fault; therefore, I must always put any issues I have and focus on my children the best I can. I have learned to speak up when I do not agree with something, but I do it with tact.

As I've said before, **honesty without tact is just plain cruelty.**

There are ways to speak your truth and ways to explain how you feel about a specific situation without attacking someone. I do not sugar coat things but will be firm when I explain how I feel. There was an incident at work, where one of my staff members was getting extremely rude text messages from our sponsor. I am very protective of my staff and even if they are wrong, I never show it in public or humiliate them, I normally will take their side, but then have a conversation with them and educate them about what they did wrong after the fact. In this incident, my staff member was not wrong, what was wrong was the way that she was being verbally attacked by this sponsor. So, I emailed this sponsor and copied her boss and my CEO about her behavior and that we didn't think that this sponsorship was the right fit for them. What was the outcome, you ask? They never emailed me back, but her CEO switched their sponsorship to another area and we only dealt with the boss the following year.

If I know I am wrong about something, I am the first to apologize. I never throw the first punch or insult, but if someone attacks me I handle it properly and be honest. I was never like this 10 years ago, if someone threw an insult or did something to slander my character behind my back, I just took it and never said anything. But, my years of experience have taught me to speak up for myself, develop thicker skin, and talk directly to the person who I feel wronged me. Which is exactly what I do. Sometimes I let the petty stuff go, but I never let the big things that conflict with my ethics and my job go, I face them head on and I am not afraid to do so because I know I am right.

Which is where my confidence in myself is most important. I should have done that from the beginning, and I am here to tell you that you must start from a young age. Do not be afraid to speak your truth and your conviction, because it will eat you up inside the way it did with me for years if you don't. I harbored anger and resentment because of how I was mistreated by my former employer and I never spoke up. Speak up during your youth, at an early age, and do it with tact. It will make all the difference in your personal well-being, your heart, and your emotional balance.

Building confidence within yourself does come with experience, but if you have the slightest confidence in yourself, use it at an early age, and help it grow. Use it the way I did in 8th grade, even though I was a nerd with glasses and braces and not the most popular kid, I still had the confidence to run for office and make a speech. Use it the way I did when facing a new high school and not being liked by my peers because I made the volleyball team without trying out. I may have been naïve, but that small confidence in myself that was instilled by my mother, I used to strengthen myself in negative experiences. Don't use confidence in a narcissistic, annoying kind of way, but use it when you know you are right about something. Being a woman with confidence and speaking up also has its disadvantages, as a woman who speaks up normally gets looked at in a negative light. But, when you have confidence in yourself and you know that speaking up is right thing to do, you should never care how you are perceived. It is said that in a perfect world (I hate when people use that), everyone would be liked and they would receive constructive feedback from peers on how to change their behavior; but like I said earlier, it's hard to educate people to change their personalities, it is who they are. I have found that when men speak their minds, they are more valued and looked upon with respect; yet, when a woman does it, we are "bitchy" and "controlling." I have never been called that to my face. I have been told that I am "sassy" or have been told to "calm down" if I didn't agree with a man. Telling a woman to "calm down" may not be the best way to get your point across.

I do consider myself a feminist. When you define feminism, it is "the belief that women and men should have equal rights and opportunities." This statement is 100% true, yet, when comparing women to men it is hard to be equal. We have different qualities than men that we can utilize in our leadership roles better than men. Men also have other qualities and strengths that women do not have. I am a woman who wants to see other women thrive, I also do not condone putting men down for us to get ahead. I have had many great men leaders that I have learned from. In my personal career, I have also never been discriminated against because I was a woman. I have always had the same rights, gone to the same universities as men, applied for the same jobs, spoken out when I disagreed, and much more. We live in a country that flourishes on women's rights and our right to speak. Women before us, who were suppressed, couldn't vote, didn't get those CEO positions, couldn't become doctors, etc, those women fought for our rights that we have now.

The Battlefield

During a war, it is survival of the fittest to stay alive, with regular, innocent human beings caught in the middle of a political or religious battleground. In order to make it out you must escape the hardships or you will become a casualty when the enemy comes knocking at your door. In consumer America, we are at war with each other, and in corporate America it is a different battlefield, it is survival of the fittest and it's a competition to make it to the top. In corporate America most people become casualties because someone else excelled faster than them at their job. Sometimes we become casualties because of tarnished reputations that are manifested about each other. It's the same battlefield we are in, therefore, why can't we as women band together and help each other instead of creating more casualties? Why have we not learned from our past, learned about women who were successful because they worked together and supported one another? Why do we have to be in an actual battlefield, one with guns and bombs, before we actually help one another?

A perfect example of women working together during war is my great-grandmothers story during the Assyrian Genocide.

In 1918 my maternal great-grandparents lived in Urmia, Iran with their newborn baby boy; my grandmother had not been born yet. During this tumultuous time, the Christian Assyrians were waiting for the Russian army to come and help against any Turkish invasion. My grandmother tells a story that is of importance to you as you move forward in your career and as a female leader. My great-grandmother endured many hardships as they escaped persecution from the Turkish army, from escaping their homeland with their baby boy to making a decision that would ultimately ruin her life forever.

You must understand the background of the Assyrian Genocide before understanding my great-grandmother's heroic story.

The Assyrian Genocide needs to be recognized world wide, but the story of the Genocide and those who lived through must be told before that can happen. "When the organization called the Committee of Union and

Progress (CUP), the "Young Turks" staged a successful coup in 1913, thereby establishing a military dictatorship on the eve of World War I." According to a study from by Jeff Benvenuto, Rachel Jacobs and John Lim, the CUP initiated a national project of "Turkey for the Turks," whereby they sought to forge a homogenous nation state through the deliberate removal of all minorities. Soon after the Ottoman Empire entered World War I in November 1914, the CUP ruthlessly began its genocidal project. Waging simultaneous genocides against Assyrians, Armenians, and Greeks, the CUP essentially followed the same pattern of group destruction. Massacres, rapes, plundering, cultural desecrations, and forced deportations were all endemic. Around 750,000 Assyrians died during the genocide, amounting to nearly three quarters of its prewar population. The rest were dispersed elsewhere, mostly in the Middle East.

According to the SEYFA Center, a nonprofit helping to promote awareness of the Assyrian Genocide and making it recognizable in congress, author David Gaunt states that "Today the ethnic category Assyrian is used for indigenous Christian peoples living in Kurdistan and northern Mesopotamia who speak (or once spoke) an Aramaic Semitic language. They were among the first peoples to become Christians and have kept ancient theologies, which came to differ very much from European Christianity. Because of language and religion, they are distinct not just from their Muslim Kurdish, Arab, and Turkish neighbors, but also from the Armenian and Greek Christians with their Indo-European languages." Gaunt also states that "by May and June of 1915, general massacres of Christians were underway and ordinary Armenians and Assyrians found themselves the focus of public contempt, being attacked for no other reason than their non-Muslim identity. Under the pretense that Assyrians refused to hand over their weapons, this period of individual harassment culminated with attacks by death-squads on villages close to Diyarbakir. As a rule, a village would be suddenly encircled, quickly disarmed and the males liquidated, the women and children dispersed."

ASSYRIANS IN HAKKARI BEFORE 1915

ASSYRIAN WOMEN IN TRADITIONAL CLOTHING IN HAKKARI, BEFORE THE ASSYRIAN GENOCIDE OF 1915

Photo credit: Assyrian_News from Instagram. Assyrian women dressed in traditional Assyrian Attire before the Assyrian Genocide of 1915.

My grandmother tells the story of her parents taking her older brother who, at the time was 5 months old, and escaping with the other Assyrians that lived in town with them. My great-grandfather put my great-grandmother on horseback with the baby and he walked alongside them. They walked and walked and didn't know where they were going until they made their way north of Iran to get to northern Iraq. She remembers being thirsty and the only way to get water was when the horses were making footprints in the mud, and as the rain filled the footprints, they would drink the water. My great-grandmother had five sisters and they all had been taken by the Kurds, kidnapped, almost certainly raped, and never heard from again. Many women fleeing, who had babies, had to make a decision whether to leave their babies behind or trek the trails of hell with their babies in their arms. My great-grandmother was faced with this ultimate decision as well when they didn't have their horse, she left her baby boy by the tree to flee, but his cries led her back to him, and she kept trekking the long trails of despair with him in her arms. She remembers women being kidnapped who were fleeing and children being slaughtered in front of them as they ran for their lives. They finally made it to Baqubah, Iraq, where the British government had established refugee camps, and they lived there for six months.

My maternal great-grandparents who survived the Assyrian genocide. Lazar and Elishwa Issa. My great grandmother pictured here.

During that time, these resilient women, who faced adversity and hardship during a time of war, as well as religious persecution and had seen their families torn apart, were survivors. As survivors of vicious attacks, they created a system within the refugee camp to help each other and their families. My great-grandmother remembers how well the British government took care of them and provided a multitude of clothing, rice, tea and other foods. The women in the camps would take these products and make the best of everything provided, and they cooked bread in Tanura (wood fire clay oven) to provide for the rest. The women worked together in this hardship and created a cohesive system to provide food, mend clothing, provide the children with rudimentary education and so much more. Sometimes, the daily food provided was so much that they didn't know what to do with the extra food. The women made sure to preserve all the extra food in case they had to be in the camps longer than expected. My great-grandmother would joke that the men would never know what to do if they were left alone with children. After six months in the refugee camp, my great-grandparents left for Habbaniyah, Iraq and they were there for several more years, and during those years, had three more boys. My grandmother was their fifth child and never endured the hardships her parents did. My grandparents, on both sides of the family, left Iraq for a better life...and here I am in the United States writing to you.

A real life superhero; a survivor; my great grandmother is pictured here in the United States at my grandmothers house.

Women working together for one goal, build. Strong women who collaborate, thrive in adversity.

As a mom of three myself, I would be confident to say that the majority of American households are predominantly run by women. According to Ericka Outland who wrote "Challenges of Women in Leadership Roles," states that even today, more often than not, with both parents working, the women run the home. So, why when looking at politics and corporations do we not see many more women in leadership roles? A quote by Lawrence H Summers – a keynote speaker – says" a society that does not establish pathways to leadership for all of its citizens is a society that is denying itself a possibility of excellence." Did you know that only 2% of Fortune 500 CEOs are women?

Let's maybe take a look at what leadership means, it may help us understand why it seems so hard for a woman to obtain it. In my opinion leadership means listening, giving back, collaborating, inspiring, delegating, communicating, influencing, creating knowledge, earning respect and the ability to constantly learn and change. The women in my great-grandmothers refugee camp fit this description and more. My great-grandmother later lost her husband after their seventh child was born and my grandmother was 4-years-old.

She was left to provide for her children on her own in a country that was cruel to Christians but tolerated them. That strength is instilled in the generations of women in my family.

According to Ericka Outland who wrote *Challenges of Women in Leadership Roles* states that "at times women play into the specific label that we are not natural leaders. Generally, we are softer spoken, more sensitive, more emotion and more of a helper. Quite often we tend to stay in the background, out of the limelight so as not to attract attention. The competitiveness in today's society is very intense. It would be nice to see more people and businesses support and nurture the differences of people rather than force them to comply."

Do we find ourselves in the battlefield to make it to the top no matter the cost? Do we change our ethics and who we are for the sake of climbing the ladder or to survive that battle? Is the workplace in America a battlefield of women vs. women? And how do we overcome this to mentor younger women coming into the workforce?

In order to survive, women must support each other and learn to mentor younger women below them without feeling that they are competition. Leaders need to help them grow and learn to become leaders themselves, instead of mediocre managers.

According to Bella St John, published author and mentor, leaders perform best when they focus on the positive. Her philosophy is based on a derivation of the management theory called Appreciative Inquiry. Basically speaking, if we equate the theory to a patch of weed-filled grass, to begin with you may have some obnoxious weeds that must be removed physically, roots and all. Once that is done, the suggestion is that we put our focus and attention on the grass, giving the grass all it needs to survive and thrive. By supporting the grass, and essentially starving the weeds, eventually the weeds either keel over or pick up and move to another patch of grass!

One of my female students once asked me "why do women often not support each other at work?" It was obviously a great question, and one that lead to an open discussion that also included the men in the class. Some of the points that were brought to our attention from the women in the class was they think that when women are in managing roles they are considered bitches, aggressive, know-it-alls, catty, gossipers, and try to sabotage other women's reputations. One of my female students shared the story of her past female bosses who were horrible to her and she assumed that is how one should make it to the top. Because it was done to her, she thought she needed to do it to others. She later learned after a staff member reported her behavior to HR that she really needed to step back and find the person she truly was in her personal life. As mentioned in chapter one, you do not have to be two different people at work and in your personal life. Be your true self and your staff will respect you. A couple of the men in my class thought that some women leaders used a lot of emotion and cry too much about everything, they nag, and are complainers.

I did have one female student tell us that her current female boss was a wonderful mentor and powerful leader for her and the rest of their staff. I asked her what qualities made her a good leader and she said "she listens and doesn't jump to conclusion right away. She doesn't gossip in the workplace and doesn't allow us to gossip. She also nurtures our positive skills and allows us to be ourselves, yet she does expect us to work and meet deadlines, no slacking off." She said her boss means business and will reprimand the staff when needed.

Caroline Turner, author of Difference Works: Improving Retention, Productivity and Profitability through Inclusion, states that we hear stories about a woman imposing higher standards on a female subordinate and determine that women are tougher on other women. The same people who report negative experiences with women, when asked, admit they have also experienced or seen women being supportive--and acknowledge men aren't always great to work with either. Turner devotes an entire chapter to helping women understand why they can be unsupportive of other women. She states that "by grasping why they do what they do, women can examine their own thoughts and behaviors and make different (conscious) choices about their own behaviors and attitudes."

One thing I admire about what Turner said is that "women tend to avoid conflict or handle conflict indirectly—and may hold onto a "grudge" for a long time. When women have a disagreement about a work issue, it can have a personal dimension. If the disagreement is with another woman bad feelings can linger. Women need to understand this tendency and try to take things less personally at work—and find healthy ways to get over a conflict." When we understand why women sabotage each other work, we can educate ourselves to learn to be the opposite and be more supportive of each other.

In the battlefield, there is competition, but it is about survival in a time of war. Your career should not be about surviving, it should be about thriving, but in corporate America it is the opposite. So why would we not be supportive each other in the workplace. If corporate America, as I say, is like a battlefield, the only way to help others, is to educate those beneath us, and support our colleagues is to work together as a team to thrive. Keep your head low, work hard, and you will be rewarded. Those who have narcissistic tendencies, the mean girls, the girls who gossip and tell on each other are the weeds, but we must focus on the positive and eventually the negativity will either change their ways or move on to another organization.

Maintain in the grass and grow, don't be the weed that no one wants to be around. If you are a leader, nurture those in your grass and let them grow by not micromanaging. Mistakes happen, but that is how one grows.

There are many challenges in being a female leader and many of them comes from outside sources, yet some come from women themselves. Yet, you must never let that deter you from growing, and you must believe in yourself as well as your abilities to be a solid leader. Being an outstanding leader means you must have confidence in yourself first. Having confidence comes from experience and years in the trenches. I know I am a great leader and I also know that I have made many mistakes to get to where I am. Another thing I know is that I still have a lot of learning to do (which is perfectly fine!). Sometimes people think that age defines your experience, but there are many young people who are very qualified to lead, they just have to prove themselves more than their older demographic.

A book by Jessica Bacal called Mistakes I Made At Work: 25 Influential Women Reflect on What They Got

Out of Getting it Wrong, is a perfect book to read if you are looking to see how other women, who struggled before really understanding and being comfortable in their own skin, learned to become better leaders. Although we as leaders still make mistakes, it is about learning from them and becoming better women leaders. In her book introduction, she states "Clearly from girlhood through graduate school, we are absorbing unhelpful messages about the many ways in which we're supposed to do things 'right' and vague advice about 'learning from mistakes.'" Bacal asks what if we heard stories about doing it wrong?

We cannot take ourselves too seriously, and those that do, I feel, are not trusted in the workplace. When you let yourself be you and laugh at your shortcomings occasionally, it shows your human side and that is what colleagues and employees want to see. They don't want to see perfection, because they know perfection can only be faked. The notion to me, "Fake it 'til you make it," is true in a sense, but how long will you be faking it for?

As I have said from the beginning of my book, my biggest mistakes and regrets were not speaking up for myself and asking for things I wanted. Even now, sometimes I have a hard time asking my boss for a raise or asking to go on more work-related seminars that I know we probably cannot afford as a County Fair. As a leader, some of my mistakes were not listening to my intuition, as a 30-year-old marketing director, I was very confident in my abilities and leadership, but I had to work harder than ever to prove that.

At the Advancement for Women's Leadership Conference I attended, motivational speaker and classical pianist Jade Simmons said to "rejoice in rejection." What? I thought to myself. I have always hated being rejected and have never liked the word "No." Yet, Simmons made complete sense when she said that rejection is better than the "Wrong Yes" and it is a "Divine delay and protection for you." She is absolutely, 100% correct. There have been many times that the door was slammed in my face or I didn't get a certain job because of timing, or I was not qualified enough, and it would bring me down.

My great-grandmother was a fierce and confident woman as a young seventeen-year-old escaping a genocide with her baby in her arms. She knew she was going to make it and she was resilient in those refugee camps and worked together with the other women. Women working together to survive, that is how we need to start thinking if we want more women in corporate America to be successful. We must support each other and not tear each other apart because one leaves early to be home with her family or because one got a raise and the other got a promotion.

That is the only way, I believe, we will thrive! It is survival of the fittest and women working together, who survive together, will make the workplace a lot brighter for the future of our younger girls.

I sit here finishing this chapter with my grandmother sitting next to me. She tells me that women in America and in today's world find (Khela go eadatokhon eale) the strength is in their hands, as translated from Assyrian, meaning women hold the power in their hands. She says, "you are educated, you have the world at your fingertips, you just have to use it the right way." She tells me that men back home didn't always treat their women with the respect they deserved and as women living in Iraq, they didn't have a voice. If they spoke, they were shut down; if they wanted to work, they were told no. My grandmother had to stay home as a child and was withdrawn from school by her older brothers to stay home and help my great-grandmother with the household as she was the only girl in the house. My great-grandfather died at a young age and her mother was left to take care of seven children on her own. My great-grandmother's strength in raising seven children by herself in Iraq needs to be commended because it was not an easy task. Although they lived in simpler times, she could not afford to send her daughters to schools and they were left to stay home. From the daily chores of cleaning, washing, hand washing clothes and living in a country where the Assyrian Christians were the minority and treated harshly, she still survived to the old age of 89 and passed away in Chicago, Illinois.

I am currently sitting here on my mother's couch as I am supposed to watch my grandmother, who recently suffered a mild heart attack and two minor strokes. When the doctors went in to conduct an electrocardiogram, or EKG, on her heart to see if she had any blockage in her arteries that caused the heart attack, the procedure caused her to have a stroke and then another when she slept. My grandmother has taken care of all of us nine grandchildren and now it is our turn to take care of her. I watch her speak and tentatively listen to every word as I don't know what her last words to me will be; which Sunday breakfast will be the last with Nana; when will it be the last time I hear one her Assyrian proverbs. As she speaks of her mother's strength and the stories of how women back home helped each other without hesitation, I am reminded of a completely different world that they lived in some 100 years ago.

Women have been liberated in America; women have come so far here that my great-grandmother would have flourished raising her children, but it would have been extremely hard for her. She would have had to compete with other women to make it to the top; not get fired and struggle to keep food on the table. My great-grandfather and my great-great-grandfather (my great-grandmother's father) had saved enough money that they were able to live on it for many years until my grandmother's brothers worked and helped financially.

There are too many demands of women now and the cost of requiring women be equal to men in the workforce at the same time making sure we maintain and raise our children "perfectly" has created a world that women are struggling to find a place in.

The War Zone: Social Media

If you think corporate America is a battlefield, social media is a war zone. Humans are social beings who need connections. The power of social media has shaped our world into smaller fragments and we can not only connect easier, but we can connect with parts of the world that we would never have been able to before. In that, I applaud Mark Zuckerberg, Tom Anderson, Jack Dorsey, and so many more who have followed in their footsteps to create a more connected world.

Although there are wondrous things about social media, there are extreme dangers. As a teenager in the 1990s and early 2000s I consider myself lucky enough not have had to grow up with social media in my face. We all have insecurities as pre-teens and teenagers, and back when I was a teenager, bullying usually occurred by someone name calling, passing notes about you, calling your house phone and hanging up, or tire slashing, etc. Thank goodness we didn't have social media when I was in college either, I couldn't imagine the photos being posted and friends tagging me at places I shouldn't have been at.

With social media becoming an integral part of our younger demographic, it is more imperative now than ever to educate them about the dangers of social media and how posts or tags could affect their future employment as well as their career. Some employers not only Google search applicants, but also look through a potential employee's social media accounts if their privacy settings are set to public. If you do have privacy settings set to "private" and not "public" and an employer asks permission to look through your social media accounts, it is your right to tell them no, as it is private. It is very rare that an employer would do that, but I have heard of it happening.

According to lawyer Lisa Guerin, employers who check applicants out online run a number of legal risks. First off, an employer who looks at an applicant's Facebook page or other social media posts could well learn information that you might not want them to have. This can lead to discrimination claims. For example, your posts or page might reveal your ethnicity, disclose that you are pregnant, or espouse your political or religious views. This type of information is off limits in the hiring process, and an employer who discovers it online and uses it as a basis for hiring decisions could face a discrimination lawsuit.

Guerin says that applicants are protected by privacy laws as well. If you have publicly posted information about yourself without bothering to restrict who can view it, you will have a difficult time arguing that it was private. An employer is free to view this information.

I look at social media like a knife. Would you ever let your seven-year-old child hold a knife without teaching them how to hold it, not to run with it, how to properly cut with it? As a mom of three, yes, I know I would give instruction and take every safety precaution necessary. Therefore, why would we not take the proper channels to properly train and educate our kids about not only the dangers of social media, but also how to properly utilize this tool. Knives can be great tools for cutting boxes, making food, carving pumpkins, slicing bread, and so many other wonderful things. Social media is a wonderful tool as well when used in the proper ways. We keep in touch with families, we debate at times about politics and life, we post photos of our children so our friends and family can like and comment about how precious they are, we click on events that we wish to attend and have social media remind us on our calendars, we can get our news, disaster relief support, traffic alerts, earthquakes that just occurred (this is for California folks who tweet about the earthquakes they feel), and many other things.

In my opinion, schools around the country should have a curriculum on how to properly use social media and be a responsible digital citizen. There is a lot of information on the Internet, yet there is inadequate teaching about social media. As parents, it is our job to educate our children at home about the dangers social media, and the internet in general.

Suicide is the 2nd leading cause of deaths among teens. Children ages ten and older often have social media at the palm of their hands and with a snap of a photo or a click of a button, cyberbullying has become an extremely dangerous part of teenager's lives, which plays a huge part on their insecurities.

According to Psychologist and CEO of the Technology Wellness Center Dr. Lisa Strohman, the United States suicide rates for middle school students doubled from 2007 to 2014. Dr. Strohman also says that many suicides can be linked to the constant use and exposure to technology. She shares an alarming new statistic: the average age a child gets their first cellphone is at six years old. Dr. Strohman goes on to explain that the bombardment of tech in our children's lives "pulls them away from interpersonal relationships, empathy, understanding how to interact with others and they're getting this constant negative data from friends, [who are] judging them, making fun of them. It is really terrifying."

According to the article "How Using Social Media Affects Teenagers" by Rachel Ehmke, experts worry that the social media and text messages that have become so integral to teenage life are promoting anxiety and lowering self-esteem. Dr. Steiner-Adair agrees that girls are particularly at risk. "Girls are socialized more to compare themselves to other people, girls in particular, to develop their identities, so it makes them more vulnerable to the downside of all this." She warns that a lack of solid self-esteem is often to blame.

"Adolescence has always been a self-esteem minefield. But today's teenagers struggle with uniquely modern attacks on their mental health. Social networking sites makes it easier for bullies to hide behind avatars and harass their victims well past school hours. Popularity is now quantified by the number of friends, likes, and comments one garners, all of which are open to public scrutiny. Add that to the usual pressure from parents, teachers, and an increasingly competitive college admissions process and you've got a powder-keg of angst."

Ehmke states that this infection has given rise to suicide clusters (defined as an unusually high number of suicides in an area in a short period of time) in some communities. In Ehmke's article she states that between 2013 and 2015, 29 kids in one Colorado county, many from just a handful of schools, had killed themselves. Palo Alto saw two suicide clusters within the last seven years. Three teenage girls in a suburb of Washington, DC committed suicide within three months of each other, an alarming rate for a county that saw only 13 suicides among girls between 2003 and 2013.

I discuss teen suicide and depression on the rise because education needs to start with teenagers first before they become young adults, in college, without knowledge of the dangers of what to post and not post before and how it hinders their potential futures.

Before you start posting your drunk bar hopping photos with your friends online or have negative comments about your present employer, you need to think twice. According to CareerBuilder.com, 70 percent of employers use social media to screen candidates before hiring, up significantly from 60 percent last year and 11 percent in 2006. Employers aren't just looking at social media – 69 percent are using online search engines such as Google, Yahoo! and Bing to research candidates as well, compared to 59 percent last year. About 57 percent are less likely to interview a candidate they can't find online and 54 percent have decided not to hire a candidate based on their social media profiles. Half of employers check current employees' social media profiles, over a third have reprimanded or fired an employee for inappropriate content, according to CareerBuilder.com.

An acquaintance of mine once posted a complaint about her job and her boss on Facebook letting her followers know how horrible her boss was. She went out of her way to even mention some colleagues, which not only threw them under the bus, but created a great deal of heartache for herself when Monday morning rolled around. You have to understand this was in 2008 when social media wasn't as popular as it is now and employers were not monitoring what you may be saying publicly about them. Yet, her colleague that was mentioned on the post told their boss so she herself wouldn't get in trouble and my acquaintance lost her job over it.

Have you also heard of Justine Sacco? The infamous tweet that went viral. Justine was headed on a 11-hour trip to Africa and as she boarded her plane she tweeted *"Going to Africa. Hope I don't get Aids. Just kidding. I'm white."* By the time she landed, the company she had worked for had fired her and her name had been tweeted 30,000 times and the hashtag #hasjustinelandedyet was used over 100,000 times.

Another example of an extreme social media blunder is Connor Riley, a 22-year-old recent graduate who bragged about being hired at Cisco on Twitter and insulting the company at the same time. *"Cisco just offered me a job! Now I have to weigh the utility of a fatty paycheck against the daily commute to San Jose and hating the work."* An employee at Cisco saw the tweet, reported it to HR, and he was never hired at the company.

With these small examples of real life people who got themselves in trouble through social media, you must be careful now more than ever what you are posting. We see celebrities getting themselves in trouble all the time or being fired from a show because of their outrageous comments on social media. You may think it is our First Amendment right to free speech, but it is also the company's right to not hire you should you make offensive comments about the company or its employees.

Use social media properly by connecting with friends and family. It is ok to have your true authentic voice, but be careful about being too extreme with politics and religion on social media.

"Social media websites are no longer performing an envisaged function of creating a positive communication link among friends, family and professionals. It is a veritable battleground, where insults fly from the human quiver, damaging lives, destroying self-esteem and a person's sense of self-worth."

- Anthony Carmona

One of the best things you can do for yourself on social media right now is opening a LinkedIn account. LinkedIn offers work networking opportunities from various companies that can get you hired. Create a profile and start putting together your resume through LinkedIn. Many companies are now asking to see your LinkedIn profile and want to see your references online, who you are connected to, your skills, published work, awards, and much more. I tell my students to create a profile even if they don't have work experience; they need to connect with their professors and put any volunteer opportunities they have done in the past as well as any computer skills they have.

I have worked hard to build a professional LinkedIn account and have connected with current and former colleagues, community members, and company CEO's within the region I live in or other high-profile companies. I was looking for remote work and applied for a high-profile company. I connected with the hire manager and recruiters from that company to introduce myself. Within a few weeks of meeting them through LinkedIn I got a job interview! The remote job did not work out for me, but I still made a connection, and should they need any other remote work, they know to contact me.

The First You

Working at a bank during my college years was one of the best work experiences I could have had at that age. It taught me how to be responsible, how to deal with customers, the importance of great managing, the true value of money and trust, and that first impressions are key. I had worked in the banking industry for over five years as I got through college and by doing this I made sure I had something to put on my resume at a young age. I will never forget my first year at the bank as a teller at the age of nineteen. One time, I recall, I was helping an older gentleman deposit money into his bank account. As I was typing on the computer and counting his money, he didn't say much. This older gentleman kept looking at me and then down at their money, and I didn't think much of it, as most customers do the same when being helped. The majority of the time I would spark a conversation with our customers and, depending on the customers mood, sometimes I didn't interact much but smiled and helped them quickly instead. This time, the interaction was minimal and this gentleman seemed like he didn't want to talk much, so I focused on my work instead. Once I was finished counting his money to deposit and the transaction receipt was printing, he said to me, "you know in my day, women who worked as tellers would always make sure they had their nails polished nicely or they didn't have any nail polish at all." I looked at my hands and was extremely embarrassed and irritated that he had the audacity to point out my chipped red nail polish on all ten fingers. He continued, "I don't want to make you feel bad, but first impressions are everything in this world, and as a teller of this bank you are representing this bank, which means you should always make sure you are polished nicely. Either you have nail polish or you don't have nail polish. We, customers, are looking at your hands when you are handling our money, which means I need to trust those hands."

"Oh my God! Was this man for real? We are not in a century that should be thinking this way," I thought. My nineteen-year-old self could not comprehend that this had just happened. I told my mom that night when I got home from work and even though she said in Assyrian "Khoosh azel talep," which means "He Can Go to Hell," in her other statements she did have to agree with him. Ever since that day, I made sure my nails were either

polished nicely with no chips on them, or that I had no nails polish on. If there is a moment where my nails are chipped, I have a complexity and anxiety that my nails must be polished nicely. During all the remaining years that I worked at the bank, I always made sure I had "honest" hands, whatever that meant to him, but to me it meant a well-kept appearance.

I have taken his words with me, and nineteen years later, I view them as words of wisdom. I didn't appreciate them then, because it made me self-conscious and he gave me unsolicited advice. My teenage self had a lot of pride and, looking back, I could see why I resented it, but my eagerness to prove someone wrong about me and the thought that I may not have "honest" hands was unbearable for me at that time. These days, the words about "honest" hands don't mean as much to me as the words "first impression," those have always stuck with me. We had strict clothing guidelines at the bank: No jeans, no spaghetti straps, no open toe shoes, no tights, no short skirts, no shorts. Everything we wore was business attire and we had to look presentable in front of the customer. Yet, there was nothing about chipped nail polish - Ha.

I had many knowledgeable branch managers and assistant managers that I learned a great deal from as well. One in particular was our assistant branch manager, who was also female. She was strict but was very nurturing to us young adults working under her. I learned a great deal about managing with finesse and managing others while respecting them. If we ever did anything wrong or our drawers didn't balance that day, there never was any condescending tone from her, she would talk to us individually to try to help us and show us the correct way of doing something. Those first few years under her guidance taught me how to respect staff while making sure they all met their sales quota and maintained their drawers properly.

Now that I think of her, I don't ever recall her ever yelling or disrespecting anyone she worked with. She was the first female leader that I had and I respect her immensely. First impressions were very important to her, and when I told her about my chipped nails, she smiled at me like a mother would and she told me he was right, but she assured me that I looked my best, so not too worry too much about it. Although, she as my boss told me not to worry too much about it, I still changed my habits and made sure to look my best every day.

As I got older and started teaching college aged students, I soon realized that some students have never been taught to dress appropriately for job interviews or even when making a presentation. Because I teach speech courses at our local community college, my students must dress business casual during their speeches. I tell them that, as much as I hate saying it, our world revolves and makes decisions based on first impressions. We must fine tune ourselves and wear appropriate clothing to be taken seriously.

First and foremost, you must know a number of things on etiquette and table manners to be prepared for interviews and later work meetings. Wearing appropriate attire to interviews will either make or break your interview. I once had a young lady come in ripped jeans and a blazer jacket with platform high heels, thinking it was appropriate. In another interview, I had a male interviewee come in wearing a baseball cap and jeans to the interview. *"Had they never been told how to dress?"* I thought. It is very rare that I come across these types of people, and the majority know to come in business attire for an interview. You don't need to spend much money either, as a nice knee length skirt with a button up shirt would work perfectly. You can wear slim high heels or business attire flat shoes. I wouldn't suggest wearing platform high heels, as you aren't going out to the nightclubs. Be simple and basic; don't overdo your make up either, I would recommend just highlighting your natural beauty; no need to contour your face for the interview, no one is doing a photoshoot.

Once you come in for the interview, make sure you arrive five to ten minutes before scheduled time. Bring samples of previous work and a copy of your resume, this shows you were prepared and make sure you have done your homework about the company. I had one woman interview for a marketing position and had never been to our county fair, but had read all of our media releases, went through our website, and followed our social media accounts just be familiar with the fair. The ones that don't make an effort and don't put in time to dress appropriately are normally the ones I never hire. Once you arrive and the employer is walking up to you, stand and make sure you have a firm handshake. When I say firm, I don't mean break their hand, just enough slight tightness so they know you are serious about the position. In one of my meetings with a sponsor, who was a veteran and served in the Air Force, I came in to shake his hand, and as he is in his eighties and I didn't want to shake too hard, I shook softer. He told me I had a weak handshake and to shake it harder. I jokingly told him that I don't like people who shake too hard. Him and I hug now when we see each other, and he often teases me about the hand shake. I normally don't give an extremely tight handshake, I think when people do that, they want to make it known that they have some power over you, to intimidate you, or some may feel that too tight of a handshake is a little "threatening" or invading too much of their space. Have you seen President Donald Trump shake someone's hand? Google it. To me it's more of an invasion of space and he wants to make sure they know he is the boss. Moving on! Slight tightness to the hand shake, look them in the eye, smile and tell them "it is a pleasure to meet you" if you haven't met them yet before.

It is normal to be nervous during an interview, this is what will set you apart from everyone else. Let your adrenaline rush work in your favor, and be yourself. Refrain from using any type of profanity or slang language. But, let your personality come out. If you are a bubbly person, don't shy away from showing that. If you are normally quiet and feel like you need talk excessively, be respectful with your answers but don't feel the need to ramble. When I hire my staff members, I look for authenticity and humbleness. I look for down to earth people that would be a stellar fit for our department. I can train anyone to do marketing, social media, and to write a press release. But, I can never change someone's personality, nor would I want to. Therefore, I make sure I hire the people who are themselves during the interview, who show me who they genuinely are. I have quiet, hard working staff and then I have outgoing, talkative staff. I also have one who is a spit-fire and tells-it-like-it-is, but the one thing they all have in common, is that they are humble, with a team working attitude.

Once your interview is finished, make sure you have questions for the employer. Always have at least one or two questions to follow up. This will make the employer know that you are curious about the job and the position.

Some questions you may ask the interviewer is *"what do you like about the company?"* or *"what are some examples of day-to-day responsibilities associated with this job?"* Another good question to ask is *"what are some opportunities and challenges facing the company right now?"* When you leave, I highly recommend you thank the receptionist or front office staff who checked you in, and write or email a thank you letter to the employer who interviewed you. A written letter for me always seals the deal, it really speaks volumes for them going out of their way in these times, where they must purchase a card, write it, then purchase a stamp and send the letter. Most times the old-fashioned ways still work in making impressions last forever.

The best interviews are those that are more like a conversation. They ask questions, you ask questions and everyone's a little more at ease throughout the process, which is why it is essential to be yourself. During the interview process, your interviewer may have Googled you or looked at some of your social media accounts if they are not set to a "private" account setting. You may look great in the interview and have done all the correct things etiquette wise, but if you had just posted photos of your drunk weekend in Las Vegas with hashtag #WildDays or #WhatHappensInVegasStaysInVegas, your interviewer may have a negative impression of you. Because one thing is, when you post photos of your weekend in Vegas, #NeverStaysInVegas. This could #RUIN your chances at getting hired!

Just like the importance of first impressions about your personal appearance and etiquette when seeking a job, you must also brand yourself positively through social media. As I've said before and will say again, many people who want to get to know you will research you through the internet. When they are researching you or when researching a company, they are looking for a perception about that brand. Presenting yourself in a consistent and positive manner will not only help you control your personal brand but it will also build your reputation.

You may be asking, what is a personal brand? Well, we are all brands. I'm a brand; I'm Adrenna, I like certain things, I look a certain way, and people know me based on how they perceive me. According to Kevan Lee in an article Buffer Social, a personal brand is the process of managing and optimizing the way that you are presented to others. McDonald's and Nike are brands, I know that when I drive by the big McDonald's sign with the letter "M" with my kids in the car, they yell for a Happy Meal because they get a toy, and majority of consumers know their tagline is "I'm lovin' it." When I purchase Nike shoes, do I "Just Do It" because they make my feet comfortable or do their shoes make me feel empowered as a woman. Whatever your reasons for making a purchase with of brand and not another, depends on your personal perception of the company.

This can all apply to personal branding on social media. I talk about being authentic in the workplace and being yourself in an interview. In my opinion, you should be the same on social media. You don't have to shy away from voicing your opinion on an election or your religious matters, because those opinions are what make you. You do, however, need to refrain from profanity, attacking another person's views; tasteless photos of yourself on social media, and airing out your family's dirty laundry; unless this is the brand you wish to display. Professional encounters require that you limit self-disclosure, because keeping some things private is different than completely having a false persona on social media.

Go to a search engine and type in your name. Are you happy with what pops up? Click on images, do any inappropriate images come up? If so, you need to start deleting and if you are not happy with what is in the search results, you have a lot of homework to do. Start the process of fine tuning your personal brand now before you start looking for your next career move.

Every year I go to the South by Southwest (SXSW) conference in Austin, Texas and every year I make sure I fine tune my LinkedIn profile before I go. I network with so many people during the conference and every time, the first thing they ask is to look at my LinkedIn profile. LinkedIn is one of the most effective and leading personal branding social media networks for business professionals. The virtual professional network has morphed from an online resume and networking site to a comprehensive personal branding resource. If you do not have a LinkedIn profile, you need to start one now. Update your resume and start making connections with professors, friends, family, as well as past colleagues.

The best part of LinkedIn is making connections with hiring managers when seeking a specific job. You can message the managers about the job and they can look at your skills, endorsements, awards, and other accomplishments without asking for your resume. Many people have been directly hired through LinkedIn. According to allbusiness.com, a good personal brand increases your name recognition, increases your reputation, gives you credibility, and establishes you as an expert in your niche.

Just remember that when you go grocery shopping and you are picking out fruits, what type of fruits do you take? Normally we look at the fruits and take the ripest, no bruises, and we normally pick out the best fruit based on first impressions. When we come home and start peeling the fruit is when we realize the fruits actual color, taste, and ripeness. Although, we hate to admit that first impressions are how we judge people, but in all reality, it is human nature. It is not until we hire and get to know our staff if they are the right fit or vice-versa; sometimes you might think you just landed the perfect job with the perfect boss, but until you start working with that boss, you won't really know their true intentions.

Conclusion

Real life superheroes don't just wear capes every day, but they can pack a real punch with determination, a lot of tenacity, and with real hard work they set a tone for younger females to make their career and achievements attainable. Comic book heroines embrace ambition and never hide from it, they are also not afraid to grow and flourish. They are selfless and take action to help those in need.

"I have yet to hear a man ask for advice on how to combine marriage and a career." - Gloria Steinem

The words from journalist, social political activist, and American feminist who was a leader and activist for the feminist movement in the late 1960s and early 1970s, Steinem spoke these words many decades ago. Yet, here we were in the 21st century still struggling to maintain a balance in work and life. My grandmother would say that women will always be fighting for equality and fighting to balance their work and life. She believes that because God created a woman second and she deceived Adam and God in eating the forbidden fruit from the tree, God cursed us women. *Cursed? No way.* I don't believe it for a second. Again, my grandmother comes from a world where women were segregated, had to stay home and raise their babies, cook, and clean. She didn't finish school so she could help her mother in the house and sadly, my grandmother still cannot read English. Yet, what her mother did during the Assyrian Genocide in 1918, and all the women who helped each other during the six months they were held in the refugee camp in Iraq, was strength and belief in themselves that has been passed down through generations.

My great-grandmother's ability to survive the Assyrian Genocide and later survive her husband's death with seven children to take care of is more determination and strength than what I have to muster to endure in this modern era. We must remember the women in our past who endured so much hardship and how they overcame their negative experiences, so we may learn from them. My grandmother may not know how to read or write English properly, but she raised a family full of strong women. Her daughter, my mother, is one of the strongest women I know. She raised all four of her children and didn't work, making sure we were taken care of at all times. Once all four of us had reached our teen years, she started working and pursued her passion for baking. My mother finished culinary academy and became one of the leading cake decorators in our town. When I started college, my mom became an entrepreneur and opened her own bakery that thrived for years. As the economy took a spiraling down turn, so did her bakery and she had to close it. But that didn't stop her! She rented a kitchen and would take orders, and she continued to be a leader in her industry.

The notion that "Women Can Do It All" is very true. We are sharp and extremely gifted in many ways. We thrive better under pressure and we can multitask like nobody's business. Women can have kids and have a career at the same time and women can be whatever they put their mind towards.

But... Yes, there is a but....

I'm tired! I'm tired of women telling young girls that "women can do it all" without being honest with them. I'm tired that successful working women aren't truly honest with themselves and I'm tired of the pressures from society that women have to be these perfect little creature. Whether you are a stay-at-home-mom and you do it all, or you are a working mom and you do it all. I'm exhausted!

I very much admire and look up to Sheryl Sandberg, but I recently went to speaking engagement in which she was a keynote speaker at my alma mater. Nearly everything she said I agreed with, but as soon as she told the audience full of young college women that "Women can be anything and we can do it all," my first instinct was an eye roll. I wanted to stand and shout "Sheryl, but I'm tired of this cliché. I'm tired of women like us telling young girls that they can do it all, without being honest with them." In her book Lean In, she does talk about the "Myth of doing it all" for women. In the beginning of the chapter she states that "Having It All" is perhaps the greatest trap ever set for women was the coining of this phrase… "These three little words are intended to be inspirational but instead make all of us feel like we have fallen short." I wish she would have quoted that to the young women in the audience during the conference I was at and discussed more deeply these issues that most young girls don't really think about when starting their careers.

There are times I do feel overwhelmed to "do it all" and making sure everything is perfect, but I have learned to say "no" to many things in order to scale back and give myself a break.

From PTO fundraiser to making sure my children are reading in Kindergarten, to helping my child be the best soccer player or the perfect little angel when we go out to dinner. It is exhausting to ensure my child makes no noise on the airplane or to ensure they don't kick the seat in front of them...

Are we stepford wives and do we have stepford children? NO.

Therefore, our society has to become more patient; unfortunately, society has become overly sensitive, so much so that we can't function as our true selves.

Things might get in your way, people or bosses might be toxic around you, but don't ever change who you are and don't ever let anyone deter you from pursuing your dreams. My daughter, who is in grade school, needs leaders from your generation to make empowering change and embrace her and her friends to be motivational leaders themselves. There are five keys to becoming a successful leader, and you will know when you are working with a great leader. But when I talk to some of my peers who I think are exceptional leaders, they never can pinpoint what makes them great. They are genuine and authentic in everything they do, they are inclusive and always think about their employees first. I had a colleague tell me that one of the questions they ask during a job interview is "tell me a time you were humble in a situation?" I thought, *how odd to ask this question?* Because those that most likely thought about it and couldn't answer the questions were the ones that were authentically humble. Yet, those who could talk about EVERY single time they were humble, probably weren't as authentic.

1. Being a Humble Leader

"Humility is not thinking less of yourself, it's thinking of yourself less." – C.S. Lewis.

Being a humble leader means walking the walk before talking the talk. You can talk about being humble, you can preach it all day long... but, if your actions say otherwise, then your staff will see you as a fraud. When you do become a leader, do not take your authority and make yourself feel that you are better than anyone. Treat your staff with respect!

2. Be an Effective Communicator

"To effectively communicate, we must realize that we are all different in the way we perceive the world and use this understanding as a guide to our communication with others." - Tony Robbins

"The most important thing in communication is hearing what isn't said." - Peter Drucker

Effective communicators inspire people and they can lead a team to greatness. Being a wonderful communicator as a leader is one of the key ingredients to sustaining a positive work environment. You build bridges with your staff and forge a connection with people at work through personal needs and by speaking to them based on individual desires. I had an employee once who confided in me that she wasn't happy living in the town where we were and wanted to move to Los Angeles. I listened to her, as she reminded me of myself at twenty-three and wanting to free myself of the small town. She asked me what I would do if I were in her shoes? Well, first I didn't want her leaving me (that was my selfish side), but I listened attentively and what she was telling me was that she was ready to move on from her position with me and spread her wings elsewhere. I love when my staff confides in me! It makes me feel like I'm making a difference in their lives. I talked to her about life and told her that if I were in her shoes I would move to L.A.

Being a good communicator means listening well, it means making sure your staff understands why you do certain things on a project and why you are telling them to do something, not just demanding they blindly follow orders.

3. Kindness is Power

"Kindness is the language which the deaf can hear and the blind can see." - Mark Twain

Being a kind leader doesn't mean you allow people to walk all over you. On the contrary, a generous leader knows when those boundaries have crossed and can be assertive when needed. However, a kind and generous leader will always make sure their staff takes credit as needed and offer enthusiastic praise. I look at my employees as my children! I treat them all equally fair but treat them as individuals with individual needs.

4. Accountability

"One person's embarrassment is another person's accountability." - Tom Price

A strong leader must never embarrass their staff publicly, instead they must always have their backs. I remember during a board meeting, I had completely messed up on a marketing report and my CEO quickly told the board that it was his fault for not clearly looking at the report and making the adjustments. Well, CLEARLY it was my fault, but when he did that, I had so much more respect for him. The next day in confidence, he did tell me to be careful and check things three times before making a report. He didn't embarrass me in front of the board, and he took the blame.

5. Authenticity

"Just be who you are and speak from your guts and heart – it's all a man has." – Hubert Humphrey.

Authentic leaders are truthful leaders that promote openness. These leaders know their limitations and their strengths. You do not have to be two different people at work and in your personal life. When you are authentic, your words align with how you treat others and with your actions. One thing I always look for in an authentic leader who may talk the talk, is if they walk the walk. If I observe them mistreating servers at a restaurant or their own staff during meetings, I know not to trust that person.

These five key ingredients will help you become an effective leader in any environment you are in and will earn you respect from your peers. When my daughter starts working in the real world, I would hope that your generation embraces flexibility and embraces women building together to make the working environment more innovative and accepting. I want my daughter to never feel pressured to "do it all," rather to conquer life goals at her own speed without societal pressures. I want her to realize that one day, she too will have to decide whether to be a stay at mom or a working mom, or perhaps not to have children at all, and all of these choices are exceptional and should harbor no judgement. I want her to know how to be a genuine leader, with kindness in her heart as she guides the next generation of women.

When my two sons are in the workforce, I hope your generation of women will help my sons understand how to manage women and learn the importance of women in the workplace. My sons and their friends will be your "Male Champions." Samantha Harrington wrote in Forbes Magazine that these "Male Champions" use their authority to push forward gender equality. It is important now more than ever to not compete with men, but to allow them to help us achieve our goals as women. I want my sons to be in a world where they can help and mentor females become effective leaders. I also hope my sons have learned from their hands-on father that child rearing is not the sole task of the woman, but instead a shared journey between both partners. My two sons will, if we've done our job as parents well, take these principles with them and view women as equals, and they will advocate for women in all facets of their lives.

We don't need men to save us, we never have! We've always had our real-life women superheroes amongst us. Whether it is your grandmother, who endured hardships, or your mother, who sacrificed her career to raise you, or worked long hours to put food on the table; Remember that you are your own superhero and can be a superhero to someone else.

My mother always said that the way you make someone feel, how you impacted their lives, or how you help them, will always leave a lasting impression. Women all over the world are making an impact and are making a change to better the world, real life superheroes that come in all shapes and sizes. Be one of them! Remember that Kindness is POWer and stand your ground when you know you are right, just like Supergirl and Wonder Woman do! Embody the larger than life traits the real-life women heroes before us demonstrated, and always work to be a positive force in the world. Lastly, never forget that...

Women working together for one goal: build. Strong women who collaborate thrive in adversity!

My maternal grandmother before marriage in 1949. Batishwa Issa Narso

Acknowledgments

First and foremost, thank you! Can you please take out your phone and tag me at @adrennaA on Twitter (or whatever the big social media hype is, I could be on it) telling me you are done reading, so I can properly thank you! One of the things I never thought I would ever accomplish is writing a book after finishing my dissertation. Yet, here I am, finished and feeling a bit raw when sharing so much of myself. I am a very private person and tend to not share much, yet the purpose of the book was to educate our younger generation and help anyone who feels overwhelmingly stuck.

I would like to thank my parents who brought me up to be annoyingly and constantly working on something. They helped me persevere and to my dad who helped my write my first speech in 8th grade when I was running for office. We got the communication gene from him and he is a profound speaker. To my mother, who is extremely strong in adversity. Her patience and love to educate others with genuine love and compassion is something I have always looked up to.

To my husband, who's patience always amazes me. He is the most loving and constantly supporting me throughout this journey called marriage. I wanted to thank my children who always keep me grounded, make me laugh, drive me crazy, and most importantly the reason why I am who I am today.

To my sister and her sometimes brutally honest opinions. My younger brother, who saves souls through his passion for the scripture and to our youngest brother, who saves lives as a fireman. Life would have been dull if I had been an only child (maybe).

To Bella St John for pushing me and guiding me over the months with this project, you are a rare gem and I can't wait to visit Scotland with you. My obsession of Outlander might finally be a reality. To my editor, Zak Killerman, his thoughtful insight was always appreciated. To Joanna Pomykala from LinkedIn, thank you for the countless emails and interview.

To YOU ALL! To you all who have been part of my life. To those leaders I had throughout my career, I want to thank you all. Without any of you, this book would not have come to fruition. I learned from you all.

About the Author

Adrenna Alkhas is a marketing and communication director and is a lecturer at her local community college. She created the award winning empowHER Lounge at her local Fair, which is geared towards inspiring young girls to be great leaders in our community. Giving girls the confidence to be themselves through workshops and giving them the skills needed to empower others as much as empowering themselves. Alkhas is a sucker for pop culture and loves the superhero genre along with watching Bravo TV. When she isn't reading, writing, or shuttling her children around, she is obsessed with Game of Thrones, Outlander series, and occasionally watching Pride and Prejudice over again. She graduated with her master's in communication in 2004 and received her Doctorate in Educational Leadership in 2011. Adrenna's marketing strategies and tactics have received several recognitions, the most recent being named "Publicist of the Year" by PR News. Adrenna is married and has three children.

emPOWher